You Can Have A Happy Marriage

Published in Nashville, Tennessee, by Thomas Nelson, Inc. and
distributed in Canada by Lawson Falle, Ltd., Cambridge, Ontario.

Published in the United States of America.

Unless otherwise stated, Scripture translations and
paraphrases are the author's.

Library of Congress Cataloging-in-Publication Data

Barber, Cyril J.
    You can have a happy marriage / Cyril J. Barber.
    Includes bibliographical references.
    ISBN 0-8407-3022-5 :
    1. Marriage—Religious aspects—Christianity.   2. Marriage-
-Biblical teaching.   I. Title.
BV835.B338   1990
248.4—dc20   89–49747
                                                     CIP

1 2 3 4 5 — 92 91 90

For my dear friends
Doug & Sue Corbett

Contents

Acknowledgments

The author wishes to express his appreciation to the following publishers who kindly granted him permission to quote from copyrighted materials presently held by them.

To Abingdon for permission to quote from C. E. Macartney's *Great Women of the Bible*.

To Augsburg for permission to quote from W. E. Hulme's *Creative Loneliness*, and R. C. H. Lenski's *Interpretation of the Acts of the Apostles*.

To Beacon Hill for permission to quote from J. Dobson's *Family Under Fire*.

To Cambridge University for permission to quote from G. N. Stanton's *Jesus of Nazareth in New Testament Preaching*.

To Harper and Row for permission to quote from J. Bishop's *The Day Christ Was Born*, and S. Vanauken's *A Severe Mercy*.

To David Low for permission to quote from N. Lofts' *Women of the Old Testament*.

To James Michener for permission to quote from *Sayonara*.

To Moody Press for permission to quote from D. E. Hiebert's *Personalities Around Paul*.

To Thomas Nelson for permission to quote from J. C. Dillow's *Solomon on Sex*.

To Fleming H. Revell for permission to quote from W. S. LaSor's *Great Personalities of the Old Testament*.

To Tyndale House for permission to quote from K. Wiebe's *Alone*.

To *U.S. News and World Report* for permission to quote

from M. Horner's "For Lots of Working Women, 'Price of Success Is Too High.'"

To Westminster for permission to quote from William Barclay's *Daily Bible Studies*.

To Word Books for permission to quote from D. A. Hubbard's *Is the Family Here to Stay?*

Introduction

Most of us in our pre-teen years heard the cliche, "Marriages are made in heaven." What we saw or read about as we approached adolescence, however, convinced us otherwise. Parental squabbles, a continual "cold war," separation or divorce, and perhaps secret lovers, led many to conclude that, despite the insistence of clergy in reciting the marriage ceremony that "marriage is a holy estate, divinely instituted for the good of mankind," the exact opposite was frequently the case. Consequently many in the 1960s and 70s, and even today, prefer "live-in" relationships to "lousing up their lives" by getting married.

Dr. James C. Dobson, in his book *Family Under Fire*, writes, "We have all witnessed the devastating cultural and attitudinal changes which have rocked the foundation of marriage and parenthood during the past decade."[1] And Dr. David Hubbard, in *Is the Family Here to Stay?*", states, "The problem becomes more critical every day. Marriages are breaking up; children are running away from home. One marriage in three ends in divorce. In some West Coast communities the divorce rate is 70 percent. Every year it is estimated one-half million children run away from their homes. The problem facing families today has reached epidemic proportions."[2]

Illustrations emphasizing what nearly all of us have observed could be multiplied. The question we ask ourselves sooner or later, and must answer, is: If marriage was indeed 'divinely instituted for the good of mankind,' then what has gone wrong? Why are so many people languishing in unhappy marriages? And more to the point, What can be done to make marriages happy?

I firmly believe that marriage is *not* obsolete. It is being berated by too many who are neither good partners in marriage nor reliable authorities on human relations. Marriages are successful where trust is honored, where views are shared, where companionship is treasured, and where love is given a chance to flow freely.

This book is the second in a planned trilogy. In *Your Love Can Last a Lifetime*, I sought to lay a foundation for personal wholeness by demonstrating from marriages in the Bible that when a couple enjoys an inner sense of *belonging, worth,* and *competence,* they can establish a strong interpersonal relationship without losing their individual identities. In this book I show from other marriages in Scripture that the dynamics of a mutually satisfying and rewarding relationship are to be derived from the *maturity* of the couple, the *unity* they establish in their relationship, and the unique bonding that takes place as they work toward the enjoyment of *sexual compatibility*.

On those occasions when I have been asked to teach this material in churches or to adult study groups, I have given a series of psychological tests. Where possible I have also used a control group. To the astonishment of many, there has been an improvement of at least 70 percent in all of the marriages within a thirteen-week period.

This book, like its predecessor, is intended for use by individuals or couples, or by adult study groups either in the church or in homes. For maximum success it is important for each couple to read over the material *before* coming together for discussion. Growth—personal or in a relationship—does not come automatically. The Apostle Paul clarified the process by which change occurs in Romans 12:2. It is through the renewing of our minds that we come progressively to understand the good and acceptable and perfect will of God. So reading over the material is a necessary prerequisite to a viable discussion.

Each one of us should have some growth-goal, which includes the spiritual, mental, and physical aspects of our lives. Those who have no such aim lack purpose and fall prey to mediocrity and boredom. What can happen in the life of an individual, can also take place in a marriage. Growth is not an option; it is a necessity. And it is not automatic but requires conscious effort.

To help facilitate growth, review questions have been provided at the end of each chapter. These are *not* the kind of questions designed to test a person's mental acuity. Nor are they the kind for which a quick answer can be given. They are intended for discussion, and they focus attention on issues (not personal failings) and are designed to aid in the internalization of the truth.

In order to prepare you for what follows, I would like to say a word about the people whose lives will be discussed. In 1 Corinthians 10:5–13, the Apostle Paul emphasized the divinely ordained purpose of the incidents related for us in the Old Testament. "These things happened to them *as an example, and they were written for our instruction,* upon whom the end of the ages have come" (v. 11, emphasis added).

When Paul wrote to Timothy, he said, "All Scripture [each and every word] is 'God-breathed' and profitable for teaching, for reproof, for correction, for training in righteousness . . ." (2 Tim. 3:16). His words apply to the Old Testament as well as to the New.

A failure to understand properly the nature of the biographical writings of the Bible has caused confusion to many believers. In our study of God's Word, it is important for us to notice the prominence given by the original writers to an individual's actions and words. *No detail is unimportant.* Dr.

G. N. Stanton, who has done considerable study in this area, affirms that the essence of a person's life is explained succinctly through his words and actions: "[so it is that] a phrase or a jest often makes a greater revelation of character than battles [won or lost] . . . ."[3] Our tendency is to want a more detailed, even developmental, approach from birth to the grave before we can understand an individual's personality. But this was not the way biography was written in antiquity. In this light John Howson makes the following wise observation regarding those whose names and deeds are forever enshrined upon the pages of Holy Writ:

> No religious book is less symmetrical than the Bible in its arrangement of doctrines and precepts; yet in no book is there so complete a code of faith and duty for all the varied circumstances of life. . . . In whatever condition we may be placed, light and guidance are always provided for us in the pages of the Scriptures. . . . *Sometimes through the indirect teaching of an example, sometimes through words dropped incidentally . . . sometimes by the relation of causal circumstances, which unexpectedly reveal great truths;* it is thus, in regard to very important matters, that we learn to 'understand what the will of the Lord is.' *Hence the full benefit of the Scriptures is not to be got except by patient search and close comparison. The careless reader misses much. The diligent and well-equipped student is often surprised when he finds how parts of the Bible, which seemed intended for no such purpose, are 'profitable for doctrine, for reproof, for correction, for instruction in righteousness.*[4]

The inspired writers of the Bible were vitally interested in the character of those about whom they wrote. They did not trace the development of the individual's personality from his parents, and they rarely summed up their subject's traits in their own words. Instead, they focused on ethical issues, and used indirect rather than direct methods to draw out the essence of a person's being. They also allowed the individual's words and actions to speak for themselves. I, therefore, have sought in this book to weigh carefully each term or expression under discussion in God's Word. In doing so I have frequently found important truths that have profited my marriage and can benefit yours as well.

As you read and study the following chapters, you should bear in mind that marriage is a union between two people who love each other to the extent that they will share with, serve, and support each other. If it is to be healthy, marriage is a two-way street—a give and take situation with open communication. When one partner dominates the other to the exclusion of his or her mate's interests and comforts, the vital bracing of such a union is weakened.

It is my firm belief, however, that *we all can have happy marriages,* if we will build our relationship upon the truths contained in God's Word. To that end I trust that this book will provide a catalyst for growth in your marriage.

—Cyril J. Barber
Hacienda Heights, California

1

Love's Many Faces

There's nothing in the world like the devotion
of a married woman. —*Oscar Wilde*

During the time Dr. Clarence Edward Macartney was pastor of the First Presbyterian Church, Pittsburgh, he asked his congregation to vote on the ten greatest women of the Bible. When their responses were tallied, Ruth stood first.

In commenting on this fact, Dr. Macartney expressed his surprise. Other notable women of the Bible such as Sarah, Hannah, Rebekah, and even Mary, the mother of the Lord Jesus, had been passed over in favor of a Moabitess.

"Why did so many people vote for Ruth?" asked Dr. Macartney.

This is not an easy question to answer. Ruth is not spoken of as being beautiful as were Sarah (see Gen. 12:11, 14–15), Rebekah (see Gen. 24:16), or Rachel (see Gen. 29:11). In fact, we are not given a description of her at all.

It would seem as if Ruth's beauty was internal, rather than external. In the book that bears her name—a work that can be read in its entirety in less than ten minutes—Ruth appears to possess a generosity of heart, a firm sense of duty, and an inner strength, that immediately win our admiration. She always appears to be saying or doing the right thing in the right way.

Perhaps there is another reason why people are attracted

to the person of Ruth and the beautifully written little book that bears her name. Perhaps the reason lies in what Ruth achieved. It was something we all desire. We have been told that to be successful, to get what is really worthwhile out of life, we must live life "in the fast lane." And so we grab what we can when we can, for we fear we may not have another opportunity tomorrow. As a consequence, we have become preoccupied with the meeting of our personal needs, and other people in our lives are given priority B (or C or D or Z).

The result of this type of approach is that people are treated as things, and things are treated as if they were people. Marital discord and corporate strife clutter up our earthly pilgrimage and make headlines in our newspapers. Our lives become sterile and lack satisfaction. We become frustrated and tend to become more and more preoccupied with our quest for that which satisfies, only to find that Ruth possessed it all along.

The Book of Ruth is a story of domestic love and fidelity. It comes between Judges and Samuel—two books filled with conflict and oppression, cruelty and strife. "It is a sweet interlude of peace and love in a fierce, wild chorus of war and passion. In this book not a single wicked, cruel, or licentious person makes his appearance. Here we behold the attractiveness of virtue, the beauty of sacrifice, and the winsomeness of trust in God."[1]

TESTING YOUR MARRIAGE'S "H.Q."*

Before we take up the story of Ruth, it may be well for each one of us to reflect on our marriage. How happy are we?

---

*"H.Q." = Happiness Quotient.

Now that our children are grown, Aldyth and I decided to take a long-overdue vacation to Hawaii. It included a visit to the world-famous Fern Grotto on the island of Kauai where many rich and influential people have recited their "I do's." We also learned that, for a suitable sum, couples could repeat their vows and be "remarried."

The question which came to our minds when we heard this was, How many couples do repeat their former marriage vows? Then a second question arose, If a couple suddenly found that their marriage was somehow invalid and that they were not really husband-and-wife, would they remarry the same person? Would they repeat their former promises of love and devotion, or would they take their unexpected freedom and seek another mate elsewhere?

For marriage to be truly happy, it needs to be founded upon a love that continues to grow and develop. The maturing of love is a process that begins in infancy and progresses through childhood and our adolescent years into adulthood. Unfortunately, age is no evidence of maturity. However, by taking a backward look, we may be able to distinguish in broad perspective the various stages.

An infant feels loved when his needs are met. He is helpless, and whenever he is hungry or needs his diapers changed, he will let everyone in hearing range know of his discomfort. He feels loved when all his needs have been met.

As he grows older and is able to move about for himself, he learns that there are some things he is permitted to do and some things that are forbidden. Love, at this stage, is equated with being left alone to do as he pleases. This stage continues for many years and may never really be outgrown.

A third stage may be entered into a little later. At this phase in his growth, he feels loved when people give him their undivided attention or compliment him on his looks or abilities. As this stage continues into the teen years, romantic relationships begin to develop. Now our adolescent child feels loved when he is made to feel special.

It is a sad fact of life that with many people their love remains at one of these levels and never fully matures.

The fourth stage of love, in contrast to the first three, is not centered in self. Instead, mature love achieves its highest fulfillment in giving of itself to the one loved.[2]

NEW NEIGHBORS

As we take up the story of Ruth, we find that a new family has settled on the high, level plateau of Moab. They have come from Judah, west of the River Jordan. Being farmers, and wishing to avoid the cities of Moab, they have chosen to live in the fields.

Rural people are known for their helpfulness and conviviality. It is probable that after the people of Moab have met with Elimelech and his family, they help them get settled. A wooden or mud dwelling will need to be erected, cattle will need to be cared for, ground tilled, and crops planted.

It is also quite probable that the women of Moab help Naomi. Their children will be encouraged to make the acquaintance of Elimelech's two sons, Mahlon and Chilion. It may have been on one of these visits with her mother to see Naomi that Ruth first saw Mahlon.

Having barely reached her teens, Ruth would have looked at Mahlon shyly, and only when she was sure he would not be watching her. Then later on, as they grew to know each other, Ruth may have caught Mahlon staring at her and given him a friendly smile.

An Unexpected Reaper

It is perhaps toward the end of Elimelech's first year on the high plateau of Moab, with his crops growing and soon to be harvested, that he suddenly falls ill. Whatever medical help is available proves insufficient, and death cuts him down, leaving only his body to be cared for by those who have been left behind.

In all probability, the neighbors rally around Naomi and her sons. They may have helped with the harvest and further strengthened the bonds between themselves and the emigrants from Judah. It is also not difficult to imagine some of the men encouraging Mahlon and Chilion, as these youths now take upon themselves the responsibilities of manhood.

"So Now You Want My Daughter"

With success attending their efforts, Mahlon and Chilion are able to care for their widowed mother, Naomi. Chilion, the younger son, perhaps because he is more competitive than his elder brother, is the first to marry. His new bride is named Orpah. Her father may have been one of those who had helped Elimelech and his family get settled in the land. How Chilion approached her father with his proposal, or who acted as go-between, we have no means of knowing. We do know that, in keeping with the custom of the times, a separate sleeping area was added to the cottage Elimelech had constructed.

Perhaps goaded into action by his younger brother's conduct, and encouraged by either Naomi or Ruth or both, Mahlon asks Ruth's father for her hand in marriage. How much he had to pay as a dowry, we are not told. All we know is that permission is given for the marriage, and another sleeping area is added to their home.

HOW OLD SHOULD ONE BE . . . ?

But were not Mahlon and Ruth too young to marry? And if they were too young, then what of Chilion and Orpah?

Should Naomi have tried to stop them? Should she not have persuaded them to wait until they were older?

In these times, girls married soon after puberty. Their husbands were only a year or two older. Normally the couple resided with the groom's parents.[3] Responsibilities were shared, with the newest bride doing the most menial chores.

All of this brings to the fore the fact that *age has little to do with happiness in marriage. Maturity, however, has everything to do with the joy and contentment of the couple.*

How happy, then, were Mahlon and Ruth in their relationship? Very happy! For ten years they lived together, and after Naomi's sons have died and Orpah and Ruth have been left widows, Naomi prays that Yahweh, the God of Israel, will show the two girls the same *hesed*—"steadfast lovingkindness"[4]—that they had shown their husbands and her during the years of their marriage (Ruth 1:8). Not many mothers-in-law can say that.

Hesed is the word used in the Bible to describe God's relationship with Israel as well as the relationship that can exist between people. It is a mature, steadfast, selfless kind of love; at once tender and strong, patient and forgiving. *Hesed,* in the Old Testament, finds its closest parallel in the New Testament word *charis,* "grace." *Charis* can be that which bestows or occasions pleasure, or it can look at a person's disposition from which certain acts of benevolence or thankfulness flow. It is also linked to the word *chara,* "joy."

The relationship of Mahlon and Ruth, according to Ruth's mother-in-law, had been characterized by this kind of attitude. So grateful is Naomi that, when saying good-bye to her daughters-in-law, she prays that the Lord will reward them in kind for their lovingkindness to her and her sons.

Now let us pause for a moment and allow this truth time

to percolate through our conscious thought processes. We all desire homes where the relationship between us and our spouse is mature and selfless, loving and thoughtful, supportive yet patient, joyful, and conducive to such intimacy that the person to whom we are married is at once our best friend and the one without whom life would be incomplete.

The question facing us, therefore, is a simple one: How may our marriages become more like the ones described in Ruth, chapter 1? We may have had ten or twenty or thirty years in which to build up resentments and to clog up the channels of communication. We may know our spouse so well that we can predict where his or her apathy toward any suggestion from us will lead, before we even begin a discussion.

Solving such marital dilemmas is fraught with difficulty. Answers cannot be prescribed. Principles of a happy, healthy marriage may, however, be put into practice. And over a period of time, change will occur.

To begin with, we can start listening—really listening!—to what our mate is saying. We can ask questions. Encourage one another. Take an interest in his or her activities and follow up conversations with inquiries as to how things went or what transpired.

In this connection, you may also wish to read H. Norman Wright's book *Communication: Key to Your Marriage* and his *The Pillars of Marriage*.

Second, we can practice togetherness. We can do things together like planning a vacation. We can start concentrating on meeting our spouse's needs without thinking of ourselves. We should also plan for change and anticipate beforehand how we will handle it. And above all, we should avoid power struggles and "bedroom politics." When we cannot agree, we should put the matter aside for the time being and pray about it.

In addition, we can also be ready to forgive.

The important principle for us to remember is that *the key to growth in any relationship is the maturity of the couple. Then, to a developing relationship should be added unity; and to these elements of a marriage, sexual compatibility.*

INTO EACH LIFE . . .

Henry Wadsworth Longfellow wrote, "Into each life some rain must fall." In doing so, he referred to the inevitability of suffering that we all experience. Things do not always turn out as we expect. People let us down. Our most cherished dreams are dashed to pieces before our eyes.

How, then, are we to face such vicissitudes? What is to be our response to the inequities of life? Is Stoic fortitude the only answer to the hurts and humiliation we face?

Consider Ruth. During ten years of marriage, she waits hopefully for a child. To be childless in her society is to bear a social stigma. To have many children, and particularly to bear her husband sons (Gen. 29:34), is calculated to endear a woman to her husband for life. Not to have children causes one to be looked upon as being punished for some previous sin.

How did women under such circumstances handle these pressures? Rachel threw a tantrum and demanded of Jacob, "Give me children, or else I die" (Gen. 29:30). Manoah and his wife had waited so long for a child that they had given up in despair (Judg. 13:2). Hannah, in agony of heart, prayed fervently for a son (1 Sam. 1:9–11). Ruth waited . . . and waited . . . and waited.

For ten years Ruth waited. In her society, she was expected to have children soon after marriage. There were no such things as pills to prevent pregnancy. She shared first the hopes and then the fears of those young women today who are described by their doctors as infertile.

Kaye Halverson describes how she feels in her book *The Wedded Unmother*. Hers is an eloquent plea for understanding. She deals graphically with a wife's maternal longings as well as the baffling enigma of a "romper-room" all prepared for a family and no children in it.

Under such daily, gnawing anxieties it is hard to maintain a semblance of equanimity and build one's marital relationship. How did Ruth do it? Naomi's comments in verse 8 give no hint of anything having arisen during the preceding ten years that Ruth had not been able to handle appropriately. Apparently, she did not permit her childlessness to come between her and her husband.

It would seem, therefore, as if Ruth were committed to her husband. He came first. Her personal desires were subordinated to developing *unity* in their relationship.

Part of unity in marriage involves the ability of a couple to share with one another and express their feelings openly. To do this effectively, there must be an atmosphere of love and understanding. Confidence must be built up. There must also be trust. When we disclose to others how we feel and share our innermost longings, we become vulnerable. For this reason, there must be a trust established whereby we know our confidant will honor our confidence.

For a couple as young as Mahlon and Ruth to have achieved such a relationship gives us new hope. Perhaps we, too, can begin to enjoy some of the joy and blessing, some of the warmth of sharing and empathic understanding that so evidently characterized their marriage.

THE LONG GOOD-BYE

In the course of time, however, perhaps due to some disease or epidemic that sweeps through the region, Mahlon dies. Gone now is Ruth's lover, her confidant, her friend. Gone, too, are the days when she could take his noon meal to him in the field, eat with him, and spend the early afternoon with him sheltered from the heat under some shady tree.

To be a widow, and at such a young age, with no children to carry on the family name and work the family farm, is unutterably tragic.[5]

In terms of such bereavement, it is not uncommon for the surviving spouse to express his or her loss through tears. This is natural. Tears have a therapeutic quality. They help us discharge our pent-up emotions. Then, when our period of mourning has passed, we can face life afresh.

Some tears, however, are tears of remorse. We weep over lost opportunities, misplaced priorities, hasty words, and actions that now, as we look back on them, reveal how self-centered and selfish we have been. Even in such cases, tears have a healing effect.

In time, with the passing of our grief, there comes an awareness of our aloneness. We lack the presence of a "significant other," someone who is emotionally significant to us, and we feel lonely, afraid of the future, and insignificant in our isolation.

This sense of aloneness makes us very vulnerable. Some people feel so lonely that they will do almost anything for companionship. They will give themselves to almost anyone who even pretends to care for them. They will even begin to try things or do things or go to places of amusement that a few months ago held no attraction for them.[6] They are lonely and unfulfilled and desperately want some meaningful relationship or activity to break the dreadful tedium that has come into their lives.

In this context, it is interesting to note Ruth's reaction. In the story, she is contrasted with Orpah who has also lost her husband. Both had had good marriages. Both had dearly loved their husbands and had known the blessing of being loved in return. Now, when Naomi decides to return to her hometown of Bethlehem, Orpah and Ruth decide to go with her (1:8–14). Naomi, however, tries to dissuade them.

Orpah relents and returns to her mother. Uppermost is her desire for a new relationship, a second marriage, a home, and the possibility of children. Her mother can perhaps arrange this. She, therefore, kisses Naomi good-bye.

Ruth, on the other hand, does not think of herself. Her thoughts are for Naomi. She, too, is a widow, but one who is beyond childbearing years and unlikely to ever marry again. Who will look after her in her declining years? In words of such eloquence that they cannot be adequately translated, Ruth says:

> Entreat me not to leave you and to turn back from following you; wherever you go, there will I go; wherever you stay, there will I stay; your people will be my people, and your God shall be my God; wherever you die, there will I die, and beside you will I be buried. May the Eternal kill me and worse, if anything but death part you and me. (Ruth 1:16–17, Moffat)

Ruth demonstrates her real love for Naomi, as well as her devotion and courage, by going with Naomi to Judah, even though in doing so she will face the Hebrew's pride of race and disdain for Moabites that has become proverbial (Deut. 23:3–4).

It would also seem as if the recent loss of her husband has convinced Ruth of eternal realities. The graciousness of Naomi in good times has impressed Ruth with the goodness of the God she worships. Now, in her hour of need, as she is leaving the old and the familiar for the unknown, she rejects with finality Molech, the god of Moab, and irrevocably commits herself to Yahweh, the God of Israel.

It probably takes Ruth and Naomi three or four days to travel the approximately sixty miles that separate Moab from Judah. They may have slept in caves or in the fields at night and eaten sparingly of their meager food during the day. They would have crossed the Jordan river at a ford slightly north of where it runs into the Dead Sea and then begun the arduous ascent to the limestone ridge on which Bethlehem is situated, a journey of about twenty miles.

On their arrival at the village, the women come out to greet them (Ruth 1:19–22). They are excited and make a fuss over Naomi. Ruth, however, they choose to ignore. And so this new convert, who is eager to experience the blessings of fellowship with God's people, receives a rude rebuff. She, however, shows no signs of resentment.

THE POINT OF IT ALL

In reviewing the events of this chapter, we see Ruth in three separate vignettes: as a young bride enjoying a ten-year marriage that is characterized by tender lovingkindness *(hesed);* as a married "unmother" coping with a problem she is powerless to correct; and as a young widow thinking not of herself, but demonstrating a well-developed, outgoing love for her mother-in-law.

The key element that links these three scenes together is Ruth's maturity. Dr. Frank C. Peters was right when he wrote that "Marriage Is for Grown-ups."[7] He traced the problems that frequently undermine our marital relationships to (1) our being spoiled as a child, growing up without adequate discipline, and now expecting our spouse to pamper us and to cater to our every need without our taking the appropriate responsibility; or (2) our being neglected as a child and growing up without proper supervision, with a lack of trust in others, and a deeply ingrained bent toward putting ourselves first.

These extremes lead to:

• Self-centeredness, which results in an inability to see the other person's point-of-view;

• A resentment that makes real intimacy almost impossible;

• Self-pity (either over one's past or the present);

• An inability to forgive;

• A proneness either to excuse our shortcomings or to defend our actions;

• A tendency to be argumentative or quarrelsome;

• An inability to initiate action or to assume responsibility;

• A misuse of any power or authority given us;

• A disdain for spiritual qualities (Gal. 5:22–23) and/or realities; and

• A tendency to depend upon feelings without maturely reasoning through the consequences of our actions.

These attitudes or actions are symptoms of immaturity and may eventually ruin a marriage.

It may be wise, therefore, as you continue to study this book, to complete the following brief inventory.

1. Are my spouse and I generous, do we give of ourselves to help or please each other?

    Always. Nearly always. Usually. Seldom. Never.

2. My spouse and I have a strong sense of commitment to our marriage.

Strongly agree. Agree. Mildly agree. Disagree. Strongly disagree.

3. Are my spouse and I able to discuss our views so that we can work toward a consensus and avoid arguments?

   Always. Nearly always. Usually. Seldom. Never.

4. When it comes to sex, my spouse and I are mutually sensitive to each other's needs and share a satisfying sexual relationship.

Strongly agree. Agree. Undecided. Disagree. Strongly disagree.

5. My spouse and I enjoy each other's company and set aside time each day to share with one another.

   Always. Frequently. Sometimes. Seldom. Never.

6. My spouse and I have a positive outlook on life so that we can enjoy the good times and cope with the "not-so-good" times together.

Strongly agree. Agree. Undecided. Disagree. Strongly disagree.

7. My spouse and I are united in our spiritual lives and also study the Bible and pray together.

   Always. Frequently. Sometimes. Seldom. Never.

How do you and your spouse's results compare? To what extent do you strongly agree on issues?

You may be among the few who have a good, healthy marriage. If so, then you should work to keep it that way and strengthen areas of possible weakness.

If your marriage is not now as stable or as fulfilling as you would like it to be, do not be discouraged. Change, like growth, takes time. From the studies in this book, you can begin to work on and to strengthen areas in your relationship.

After having reread Ruth chapter 1, you may wish to aid in the internalization of the message by interacting with or discussing the following questions.

Interaction

1. As you review this story, consider the decisions Ruth made: to accompany Naomi to Judah, 1:6–7; not to return to Moab even after Naomi's persuasive entreaty and Orpah's departure, 1:8–15; and her solemn avowal in verses 16–17. What do these tell you about (a) the level of her maturity; (b) her interpersonal relations; and (c) her spiritual commitment?

2. Naomi described Ruth's relationship with Mahlon by using the Hebrew word *hesed,* steadfast lovingkindness. Consider the ways in which such mature love adds to the fulfillment of a marriage. What things may prevent its outworking?

3. If love matures through four stages, what stage had Orpah reached? How did her love for Naomi differ in quality from Ruth's? Consider the place of *self* in each of the four stages. Discuss the ways in which steadfast lovingkindness can be given the opportunity to grow in a marriage.

4. What kind of a mother-in-law was Naomi to her daughter-in-law? Her conversations in the Book of Ruth reveal that she was always thinking of others, desiring what was best for them, but never manipulating them into doing what she wanted. Make a list of some of her other characteristics. Which would you like most to emulate when your children marry?

5. From Ruth 1 and the lessons it conveys, how should we handle the pressures and problems of life? Will such a method demonstrate our maturity and enhance the unity of our marital relationship? Why?

Second Time Around

It is easy enough to be prudent,
When nothing tempts you to stray;
When without or within no voice of sin
Is luring your soul away;
But it's only a negative virtue
Until it is tried by fire,
And the life that is worth the honor of earth,
Is the one that resists desire.
— Ella Wheeler Wilcox

In her book, *Alone, A Widow's Search for Joy,* Katie Wiebe relates a conversation she had with another widow soon after her husband had died:

"To be a widow is pure humiliation."
The speaker was a young widow with three small children. She spoke with certainty and yet without malice.
I stared at her unbelievingly. Surely she meant loneliness. I knew that the new life before me as a widow would be starkly empty of rich life relationships. Perhaps she meant difficulty?
A few weeks later when I was well into my novitiate as a widow, I began to understand what she'd meant. She had called it humiliation. The apostle James spoke of it as affliction. When the prophet Jeremiah wanted to describe the desolation of Jerusalem after the fall of Judah, he compared it to a widow: "How solitary lies the city, once so full of people!

Once great among nations, now become a widow" (Lam. 1:1 NEB).

To me, the death of my husband Walter meant being ceremoniously ushered out of the life I'd known and enjoyed—albeit with music and processions and guests and feasting, all draped with the black crepe of sorrow—into a completely new way of living.[1]

This description of the sense of aloneness and estrangement people feel when their lives are devoid of any meaningful relationship is not new. It faces widows and widowers in all walks of life and in all the cultures of the world. In some countries it is worse than in others, for a widow may be looked upon as *persona non grata*—a person without rights or standing in a community.

This was true of widows in Israel. Without a family to which she could belong, a widow was totally destitute. Without the benefits of life insurance, social security, or some form of steady income, she was poverty-stricken (Mark 12:42).

Widows were also very vulnerable. They could easily be exploited (Mark 12:40). To protect them, God included legislation in the Mosaic law (Ex. 22:22–27; Deut. 10:17, 18; 14:29; 24:19–22). However, as God's Law was set aside, widows were neglected. Two choices lay before them: prostitution or trying during the few weeks of harvest to glean enough to support life until the next harvest season.

CRUCIAL DECISION

As we consider the situation of Ruth and Naomi, we note that the Lord has brought them back to Bethlehem at the beginning of the barley harvest (Ruth 1:22).

Ruth sees the men and women in the fields as they climb the steep ascent from the Jordan river. An idea begins to form in her mind. The next morning she asks Naomi if it is wise for her to go and glean in the fields (2:2). Ruth is no doubt aware of the immoral practices that were common among the heathen at harvest time.[2] She, therefore, asks Naomi if it is safe. Naomi assents, even though she knows Ruth will be running a certain risk—even in Bethlehem (2:9, 22; 3:14).

The facts of the story are easy enough to grasp. Our interest lies in what we can learn about Ruth from her words to Naomi. As we take a close look at the brief conversation, three important things emerge that we will do well to observe.

Ruth is pro-active as opposed to being reactive. She has observed the reapers, reflected on the possibilities of gleaning grain in order to support herself and Naomi, and come to a decision.

Ruth is also sensible. She discusses her idea with her mother-in-law and manifests an openness to receive counsel.

Ruth exhibits a mature interdependence. Her words "in whose sight I shall find favor" indicate that she is prepared to persevere in her search for a suitable field in which to glean until she finds someone who will readily grant her permission.

When we consider that only a short time earlier Ruth had lost her husband, and that other people in a similar situation frequently want someone to lean on, we begin to see how mature and resourceful she is.

A DISCREET REQUEST

On approaching an overseer[3] in a section of the field, Ruth asks, "Please let me glean and gather [up the barley dropped by the reapers by following] after them" (Ruth 2:7). To her respectful request she receives an affirmative response.

We believe that in Ruth's attitude and conduct we have a good example of mature independence. She is gracious. Her question is direct. She is not looking for any favors. All she desires to do is glean in the field in accordance with the Law of the Lord. There is not a single hint of arrogance in her words. She shows respect for the personhood and position of the overseer. He responds by giving her permission to glean in the field.

In our culture, there is an attitude abroad that stresses a kind of aggressiveness if you are to get what you want, an insistence upon one's rights and the discarding of traditional values or courtesies. Lamentably, some of these attitudes have also been transplanted from the marketplace into the home.

Let those who are caught up in these trends observe that there is a distinction between aggressiveness and assertion. Aggressiveness is being demanding without regard for the other person's (spouse's or employer's) sense of esteem; it is insisting on one's own desires without concern for the other person's feelings. Appropriate assertiveness, however, means raising issues in such a way that the result will be beneficial to all concerned.

Ruth is appropriately assertive. She is tactful. She could have insisted on the provisions of the Mosaic law. Instead, she asks for permission to glean in the field in such a way that it enhances the foreman's sense of worth. He is flattered that she considers him worthy of such courtesy.

Inappropriate aggressiveness is, in reality, an evidence of insecurity. A person may gain his or her immediate ends by intimidation, but in a different situation, like accepting kindness, one suddenly finds one's self in an awkward position.

ACCEPTING KINDNESS

Many women whom we have counseled believe that, unless they are constantly *pushing* themselves into the limelight or bringing themselves to the attention of their employers, they will be passed over. Not so! Look at Ruth. The overseer of the workers is so impressed with her winsomeness that he watches her all morning (Ruth 2:7)! Similarly, the foreman's employer, Boaz, takes notice of her. He calls her to him, and, in words of deep sincerity, encourages her (2:8–13).

In the brief conversation between Boaz and Ruth, we notice in her reaction to his words an evidence of her maturity. She is sufficiently at ease in coming into his presence not to feel fear. For all she knows, he might have called her to him to tell her to go elsewhere. However, there is no intimation in her response that she is suddenly relieved when she finds this is not the case (Ruth 2:10). Instead, following Boaz' kind reassurance, she has only a question: "Why have I found favor in your sight . . . ?" In this we see her transparency. She is open and honest and secure enough in her own person to inquire the reason for Boaz' kindness to her.

Boaz responds by telling her that all she has done for Naomi has been fully reported to him. For this encouragement, Ruth expresses her thanks. Boaz has spoken the first kind words she has heard since leaving Moab. He has comforted and encouraged her.

All of this points to another inescapable fact. Ruth is maturely in touch with her feelings. She had evidently been hurt by the rebuff of the women of Bethlehem. She also senses her vulnerability. When Boaz speaks to her needs, she does not deny how she feels or disavow that she needs encouragement. Instead, she maturely acknowledges her inner feelings (2:13).

Further evidence of the fact that Ruth has made an impression on those about her comes when Boaz invites her to dine with him. Had her former attitude been one of arrogance, she would have been too embarrassed to accept (2:7). Her gracious manner with all whom she has met has, however, assured her of a welcome reception.

AN EVER-PRESENT PROBLEM

But what of Ruth's vulnerability?

A well-respected sociologist said, "We are all sexual beings. Wherever you have a man and a woman together, there you have a 'sexual' relationship." This does not mean that all relationships between men and women end up in intercourse. It does mean that *our sexuality is an inescapable part of our identity*. We relate to each other as sexual beings.

We find that one of the primary concerns of women in the marketplace is sexual harassment. They feel used, put upon, and sometimes even coerced into performing "favors" for their bosses or out-of-town clients. According to one survey, about seventy percent of working women experience these pressures in one form or another. We need to be sensitive to these issues and expose them where they exist.[4]

Two types of women are particularly susceptible to these kinds of pressures: the shy and retiring ones who try to repress their sexuality in the hope that they will be unnoticed, and those who flaunt their sexuality.

On the other hand, there is Ruth. She had all the disadvantages: No husband to protect her (2:5); a foreigner without "rights in Israel"; and one compelled by necessity to work in places where she could easily be "set upon" (v. 22) by some of the ribald, immoral young men who had come to Bethlehem to work in the fields. Yet, Ruth neither suppressed her sexuality nor flirted with the reapers. She was friendly, yet discreet. Later on, Boaz admits that she could have had her pick of any of the attractive young men (3:10).

How was Ruth able to enjoy the acceptance of the reapers and yet avoid the very evident dangers? It would seem as if she had established her priorities and did not deviate from them (2:23). This was harder for Ruth than for many today, for she was a woman in a man's world. In her relationship with men, however, she appears to have been friendly without offering any encouragement to anyone. She was discreet; she kept her distance and the men respected her.

"BOAZ, WILL YOU MARRY ME?"

Six weeks pass. Then, toward the end of the harvest season when the threshing begins, Naomi approaches Ruth with a suggestion. Her opening words, "My daughter, have I not been seeking the rest [marriage] for you, that it may be well with you?" (3:1), show Naomi's loving concern. They also tacitly reveal that Naomi has been checking over the men for a possible husband for Ruth.

Naomi's plan (3:1–4) has as its basis Israel's levirate, or brother-in-law, marriage as explained in Deuteronomy 25:5–10. To be sure, the parallel is not exact, for Ruth's brother-in-law would have been Chilion, and he is dead. Naomi, however, plans to act upon the principle of God's law. Boaz, of course, is the unsuspecting groom.

Ruth has not had time to prepare herself mentally or

emotionally for Naomi's plan. Naomi begins by reminding her that she has been the recipient of Boaz' favors. But how will he respond to her asking him to marry her?

THE PROPOSAL

The scene described by the author: the threshing floor, the fire at the far end, and the workers sleeping near the fire to keep warm with the owner sleeping close to the grain to guard it, were all familiar to those who first heard the story. So was the Law. Boaz could easily decline Ruth's proposal, for he was not her brother-in-law.

At dusk, in accordance with Naomi's instructions, Ruth comes to the threshing floor. She observes where Boaz lies down and, when everyone is snoring contentedly, quietly makes her way to where he is sleeping. Then she lifts up his cloak, exposing his feet to the cold night air. This done, she lies down and waits. In the middle of the night Boaz awakens and, when he reaches over to cover his feet, he finds a woman lying there.

"Who are you?" he asks.

Ruth identifies herself. Then she requests: "Spread your covering [lit., wing] over your maid, for you are a near kinsman."

Boaz' response is one of *praise*. He does not censure her for either her method of approach or her request. Instead, knowing that she is doing this for Naomi's sake, he commends her (3:10–12). He also promises to do all he can for her. He advises her, however, that there is a relative nearer of kin to Elimelech than he. This kinsman has prior responsibility.

APPROPRIATE DISCRETION

Boaz then says, "Remain the night . . .", and so Ruth continues to lie at his feet (not by his side) until the morning

(3:13, 14). Then, with fitting concern for Boaz' reputation, she arises before one person can recognize another and returns to Naomi.

There are many commentators who believe that Ruth and Boaz engaged in sexual intercourse that night. They believe that this was part of Naomi's plan and that for this reason Boaz felt obliged to marry her. The biblical text is against such a view.

More to the point is the observation of Dr. G. Campbell Morgan.[5] He states that Ruth and Boaz were "saints" in the true meaning of the word. They were *separated to the will of God*. They were people of character, intent on doing what was right. While the situation on the threshing floor constituted an opportunity for intimacy, what each was as a person precluded all inappropriate conduct.

A BRIDE-TO-BE

The next morning, Boaz approaches his unnamed kinsman at the gate of the city. This man declines marriage to Ruth, and Boaz states his intentions before the elders and the people of Bethlehem (4:10ff.).

Leaving the gate of the city, he walks to Naomi's humble cottage and takes Ruth (with Naomi following) to his home. There Ruth becomes his wife and, in the course of time, bears him a son (4:13).

But how was Ruth able to make the mental, emotional, and physical adjustments from widowhood to being the wife of Boaz? How was she able to make the transition from the discipline of the threshing floor (where she kept her sexual desires under control) to being a warm and responsive wife?

The only answer to these questions seems to lie, once again, in her maturity as a person—a maturity which enabled her to cope with rapid change. Coupled with this maturity was an ability to be responsive—with her entire being! We caught a glimpse of this in her first meeting with Boaz (2:8–13). Ruth evidenced there the fact that she was in touch with, but not controlled by, her emotions. In her marriage to Boaz, she committed herself entirely to the new relationship, proving that real love is a matter of the will.

AN IDEAL WIFE

All that Ruth was, therefore, she brought to her marriage. This included:

- Her capacity for love and devotion so evident in her first marriage;
- Her ability to be pro-active, to reach a decision, and to adjust to rapid change;
- Her willing subordination to Naomi and acceptance of her counsel;
- Her tactful assertion and graciousness in receiving compliments;
- Her modesty and discretion with the men harvesting the crops;
- Her personal restraint while with Boaz on the threshing floor; and
- Her evident enjoyment of sexual intimacy in marriage (4:13).

These characteristics commend Ruth to us as an ideal woman.

Yet, Ruth's situation as a widow, working to help support a "family," differs little from that of working women today. And seeing that, by some bureau's statistics, women constitute fifty-seven percent of the work force, there appears to be a great deal working wives can learn from Ruth's example.

Perhaps the key to Ruth's success is her mature interdependence. She was secure in her person, possessed a healthy image of herself, and was able to relate positively to people—rich or poor, landowners or servants, men as well as women—with an ease that we all envy. And when we realize that Ruth was no more than twenty-five years of age at the time of our story, her ability becomes even more impressive.

Being maturely interdependent is *not* synonymous with being either irresponsible or overbearing. Those who are irresponsible show by their attitude their immaturity through lack of discipline, while those who are overbearing become authoritarian and alienate those with whom they live and work. In Ruth, we see a quality of character that does not need power or position in order to feel fulfilled. Her character conjures up before us the image of an individual—man or woman—who knows what he or she is about, who works hard (but without undue anxiety over the future), and who is able to cooperate with other individuals (or departments) without fearing that someone else may get the credit. Their sense of fulfillment comes from within.

Few of us in our society have been reared to be maturely interdependent. Most of us fall into one of two groups mentioned by Dr. Frank C. Peters who were either spoiled as children or deprived. Consequently, there are relatively few of us who, as with Ruth, evidence true maturity.

The result of our immaturity is seen is our self-seeking. It results in a lack of unity in the home and is evidenced by our inability to relate meaningfully to others. And unless this is corrected, we will pass on to our children a model of our own immaturity. We need, therefore, an example of what we should be like, and the example of Ruth serves as an illustration of what we may become.

Interaction

1. In Ruth chapter 2, we see Ruth (a) taking upon herself the support of Naomi (for our purposes let us suppose this one to be any member of a family); (b) approaching a stranger—the foreman over the reapers—with a request for a favor; and (c) responding to Boaz' kind words and invitation to join him and his workers for lunch.

(a) Consider Ruth's ability to be pro-active. How does a pro-active person differ from someone who is reactive by nature? Are there any dangers in being too assertive? What difficulties arise when people are too passive? How did Ruth handle the situation that faced her?

(b) Discuss Ruth's tactfulness and discretion in approaching the foreman (see Ruth 2:7 for his recounting of her request). Do you think Ruth was naturally respectful? Are we given other evidences of Eastern courtesy in this chapter? How, then, may appropriate assertion be applied to the situations you face?

(c) Consider Ruth's sudden change of fortune: at one moment a despised foreigner with no man to look after her and give her dignity in the community (see Ruth 2:5), and then the recipient of favors from Bethlehem's *gibbor hayil*, "mighty [man] of valor" (Ruth 2:14ff.). How might she have reacted? How did she respond? Do you think that she was concerned about how Boaz' other servants might treat her? What does this tell us about her?

2. Read over the events described in Ruth chapter 3. Naomi evidently felt that she could trust both Boaz and Ruth, otherwise she would never have placed her beloved daughter-in-law in such an invidious position. Discuss

Ruth's sense of propriety (Ruth 3:7, 14). Consider also her request (v. 9). Do you think this is what Naomi told her to say (3:4)? Is there anything in Boaz' reply (vv. 10–13) to indicate that he realized Ruth was prepared to enter into marriage for Naomi's sake?

3. How do you think Ruth conducted herself as the wife of Boaz? Do you think she was interested only in his money? Why? Is your response consistent with Ruth's loving nature* and evident respect for personhood?

4. What mental and emotional adjustments did Ruth have to make between the events described in 3:1 and 4:13? From what you know of her and her evident maturity, how do you think she made them?

5. There is evidence in the text of Ruth 3:14—"and she rose before one could recognize another"—that Ruth was concerned about Boaz' reputation. He responds (v. 14) by being concerned about hers. How would such mutual concern for each other's well-being pave the way for the development of unity in their marital relationship? What may we learn from them?

---

*True, mature love may be defined as "always seeking the highest good in the one loved, even to the point of self-sacrifice." It was a characteristic possessed by both Ruth and Boaz.

3

Uncommon Qualities

He is not a lover who does not love forever. —Euripides

True love is the ripe fruit of a lifetime. —Lamartine

We met Karen at a Bible study in the home of some friends. We were studying the lives and relationships of couples in the Bible. Our hostess, knowing that Karen and her husband, José Petrino, were experiencing marital difficulties, invited them both to the discussion. Only Karen came.

Several weeks later, after Karen felt that she could trust us, she visited us in our home. We allowed her to tell her story. She had married José against her parents' wishes. Because of cultural differences, she felt she was only tolerated by his relatives and friends, and she knew that he was not accepted by hers.

At first, their situation brought them closer together. They had each other and did everything together. In time, two little girls were born into their home. When Marguerita arrived, Karen felt she should stay at home and devote herself to being a mother.

José, however, did not have a well-paying job. He had been with his employer for five years and had not received a raise. With doctor's bills and then the arrival of María, Karen confessed that she had begun to nag José to find something that brought in more money.

Karen admitted that José was kind to her and the children. Something, however, had gone out of their relationship. At home, José had a defeatist attitude; away from home, Karen later learned, he was really quite machismo.

In questioning Karen about her parents, we learned that her father was well-to-do, had always provided for the family, and that her mother "had never worked a day in her life."

We then probed deeper into Karen's source of the resentment and found that what she was really wanting (now that her maternal needs were being met with Marguerita and María) was a return to the security of her childhood—a "father" to provide for her.

We tried to see Karen and José together, but he refused. One night we stopped by the home. Aldyth visited with Karen and helped her with the girls, and I strolled into the garage where José was working on the car.

It did not take long to learn of the acute hurt he was feeling—rejected by Karen's parents and friends and now hurt again by Karen's constant criticisms and emasculating manner. In seeking for acceptance, José had fallen back on his earlier heritage. He had adopted a "macho" way of life when away from home. He felt affirmed when other women found him attractive. However, there was always Karen and her acerbic criticisms to be faced when he returned home. Lack of success at work and criticism at home had taken the joy out of living for José.

BIBLICAL IMAGERY

The Bible does not promise that marriage will be a proverbial "bed of roses." The Apostle Paul warned that those who marry will have "trouble in the flesh" (1 Cor. 7:28 KJV). This does not mean that marriage is devoid of all benefits. The rewards, however, are for those who work for them. For such, the home becomes a haven; the husband can enjoy the companionship of his wife (see Eccl. 9:9), and his wife can rest confidently in the love of her husband.

It is this idea of rest that is twice brought before us in the Book of Ruth (1:9; 3:1). The word *menuchah* and its cognate *manoah*, both rendered "rest," look not at financial ease or comfort, but at the union of a man and a woman, and the trust and confidence each has in the other. It brings before the mind the emotional completeness of both parties, the sense of security they feel in each other, and the enjoyment they derive from the uniqueness of their relationship.

This kind of rest is not for those who are in any way immature. It involves an acceptance of situations that cannot be changed and a willingness to work together on all areas of mutual concern.

The question before us in this chapter, therefore, is a simple one: What kind of man can provide this kind of rest for the woman who becomes his wife?

FIRST IMPRESSIONS

Students of the Scriptures are generally agreed that Ruth stands out on the pages of God's Word as an ideal wife. Can it be said that Boaz is an example of an ideal husband?

We are abruptly introduced to Boaz by the writer of the book. He gives us a brief statement about him: "Now Naomi had a kinsman of her husband, a mighty man of valor,[1] of the family of Elimelech, whose name was Boaz" (Ruth 2:1).

Boaz had apparently achieved recognition for his service to the little village of Bethlehem and had been given the title *gibbor hayil*, "a mighty [man] of valor."

Because Canaanites from the surrounding area or Bedouins from the Negev made periodic raids on unsuspecting villages, it was necessary for farmers to protect their live-stock and crops. Boaz had evidently distinguished himself as the leader of Bethlehem's little band of militia. He had proved himself to be a man of resourcefulness and courage.

The writer of this story draws attention to Boaz a second time in Ruth 2:4. His words are abrupt. "And look, Boaz came from Bethlehem. . . ." He obviously desired his read-ers to form a lasting impression of Boaz, or else he would not have used this literary device.

Personal Piety

Boaz is characterized by a personal piety. Had we not already been told that he was a brave and capable man, we might have come to the erroneous conclusion that he was really a Casper Milquetoast who was too weak to amount to much and wore his piety on his sleeve.

Such, however, is not the case. Boaz' strength of charac-ter is beyond question. He is also a godly person with a faith to match his physical prowess.

Notice, too, Boaz' influence on his workers. He greets them in the name of the Lord, Yahweh,[2] the covenant-keeping God of Israel, and they reply in the same vein (Ruth 2:4). The men and women harvesting the grain evi-dently respect Boaz sufficiently to defer to his beliefs. His greeting, so natural and so unaffected, is in effect a testi-mony to the grace of God in his life.

It is easy to pass over this greeting and think of his "May Yahweh be with you" as little more than a cliché. It was not.[3] However, the important point for us to remember is that only in Judaism and Christianity does power lie in the ability to bless. In all pagan religions, as well as pagan practices performed under the name of "Christianity," power lies in the ability to curse, punish, or coerce. Boaz' desire for the good of his workers stands in marked contrast to the punitive, manipulative, or oppressive practices of others who did not share his spiritual convictions. As such, he sets a worthy example for men in business today.

Personal Kindness

Notice, too, the personal interest Boaz takes in Bethlehem's poor. As he looks out over the field, he knows those whose impoverished circumstances bring them back to his portion of the field year after year. Then he observes a stranger. He has not seen her before.

"Whose young woman is this?" he asks his foreman.

"She is [the] young Moabite woman who returned with Naomi."

Boaz responds to this information by calling Ruth to him. The Hebrew idioms of verses 8–9 are the Semitic way of stating something in a positive manner. Read in terms of their real import, Boaz is seen as affirming and encouraging Ruth! He also facilitates the work she is doing by giving her permission to slake her thirst from the water drawn from Bethlehem's well by his young men (1 Chron. 11:17–18).

We should notice that Boaz is kind to Ruth without being patronizing. He is helpful without being condescending. He makes it possible for Ruth to receive maximum results from her efforts without depriving her of the dignity that comes from honest toil.

In addition, sensing that Ruth has had little to eat, he invites her to join him and his workers for the noon meal (Ruth 2:14–16). Knowing how easy it will be for his workers to ill-treat her, he serves her himself. In this way he shows his servants how he expects them to treat her. He also gives her more food than she can eat so that she has some left over to take home to Naomi.

By his actions, Boaz shows himself to be kind and understanding, God-centered and other-directed. He is concerned for the poor and demonstrates by his example the best way to help and assist them.

Personal Affability

Another characteristic of Boaz that we do well to note is his ability to enjoy life. As we read these chapters and observe him in his relationship with others, he appears to be large-hearted and affable, capable of enjoying the blessings of the Lord and desirous of sharing them with others. He does not separate himself from his workers, but eats with them. And later on, when the harvesting is over and the threshing begins, he feasts with them. He evidently is the kind of person who does not feel the need to set a distance between himself and those who work for him.

We need to keep in mind, as we consider these verses, that the people of Israel had just come through a time of severe famine (1:1, 4, 6). The poor, who had little or nothing to lose, somehow survived. The rich had lost much of their wealth and now might wish to regain as much of their former riches as possible.

Boaz, we know, is not a wealthy man, for in chapter 4 the elders pray that, on account of his loyalty to the teaching of God's law, he "*may achieve wealth* in Ephrathah [the ancient name for the district in which their city was situated] and become famous in Bethlehem" (4:11). Instead of exhibiting a greedy, grasping spirit, we see Boaz as magnanimous and generous, kind and considerate, and in every way the kind of man who draws out the best in people.

NO COMPROMISES

As we consider the events described in chapter 3 from Boaz' point of view, we read that it is to his threshing floor that Ruth comes with her request that he marry her (3:7–13).

Boaz has had no prior warning of this visit or of Ruth's proposal, and, therefore, his response is most revealing. He praises her for wishing to marry within the family of Elimelech. In addition, he admits the legitimacy of her claim. He could have insisted on the letter of the law and excused himself from becoming involved, because he was not her brother-in-law, but only a relative of her late husband (Deut. 25:5–10).

Marriage = Commitment

Instead of seeking for a way out, Boaz adheres to the gracious intent of the Mosaic law and agrees to marry Ruth. There is a problem, however; another relative, nearer of kin to Elimelech than he, has the prior claim. With an openness and candor that reveals Boaz' basic integrity, he advises Ruth of the existence of another kinsman.

In the morning, Boaz goes in search of Elimelech's unnamed kinsman and advises him of his rights (Ruth 4:1–6). He even recommends that he buy Naomi's land. He then advises him that it will also be necessary for him to marry Ruth.

When this relative declines to take Ruth as his wife, Boaz states his intentions. He will not only marry Ruth, but their first son will inherit the estate Naomi is forced to sell (vv. 9–10).

For Boaz, the path of duty is clear. Knowing the teaching of God's Word, he adheres to its spirit, marries Ruth, and takes Naomi into his home as well (vv. 16–17). In all of his actions, he shows himself to be an honorable man.

A Time for Love

In recounting the marriage of Ruth and Boaz, the biblical text is very brief (4:13). It contains only the essentials of what transpired. What it leaves unstated is that, in Boaz,

Ruth had found her *menuchah*, rest. He was the kind of husband she could trust, in whose love she was secure, and on whose provision for her and her children she could rely.

This does not mean that marital rest frees a woman from all problems, trials, or difficulties. Unfortunately, the harsh realities of life remain. It does mean that, in marriage, a husband and wife find comfort and encouragement in each other. Their anxieties are reduced and, hopefully, their joys are doubled.

IS THERE AN IDEAL KIND OF HUSBAND?

Our entertainment media has portrayed the ideal man as young, athletic, slim, and single. Yes, single! He is the kind of person women can "fall in love with" while watching him on the TV screen. And being single, he is also available.

The entertainment industry has also programmed us for temporary relationships. The "ideal man" of many of the TV serials has a relationship with one beautiful woman each week . . . (until the summer months when we watch reruns and wait expectantly for the Fall Preview to see if our favorite show[s] will be continued).

Because real life is as different from the Hollywood stage as Lake Tahoe is from the Painted Desert, we have difficulty adjusting to "the real thing"—marriage to the man we married. For this reason, we need to take a closer look at Boaz. He comes to us across the centuries as an ideal kind of man; and all that he was as a man he brought to his marriage to Ruth.

Unaffected Strength

Boaz did not need to try to project a special "male" image. He is described in our Bibles as a man who was comfortable in his role as a man. Look at the record again. Boaz had . . .

- *A strong sense of autonomy.* He was able to make decisions; to relate to a variety of people; and demonstrate his ability to graciously and tactfully handle an assortment of different situations.
- *A healthy view of himself as a man.* He could, therefore, conduct himself appropriately before his servants as well as the elders of the city. At no time does he give any evidence of needing to enforce his authority. In addition, when Ruth came to the threshing floor, he treated her with respect. As Dr. D. B. MacDonald has noted, "Boaz is shown quietly handling the situation [in chap. 3] like a gentleman, and not either as an old fool or a village lout."[4] Yet when circumstances changed and he married Ruth, he initiated and participated in sexual intimacy with her. When necessary, therefore, he could exercise restraint, and when intimacy was appropriate, he could enjoy it.
- *A well-defined, internalized morality.* He was aware of the seedy side of human nature (2:15, 16), yet not prudish; he was honest in his dealings with his near-relative (4:1–4) and steadfast in his determination to do what was right (even when this involved having his firstborn son legally adopted by Naomi and succeeding to Mahlon's estate).
- *A comfortable acceptance of his "career choice" as a farmer,* yet possessed the flexibility and versatility to lead Bethlehem's militia and also conduct legal matters at the gate of the city.
- *A sense of destiny in trusting in God's plan to recompense the righteous.* He was prepared to do what was right, even if it meant personal privation. In Boaz' case, his future

orientation was underscored in the benediction of the elders (4:11–12) and also by the writer (who links *his* name, not Mahlon's, to David; see vv. 17, 18–22).

Being mature in his person, Boaz was therefore free to be himself. As occasion required, he could be brave and resourceful, sociable and kind, good-natured and affable, reserved as well as able to enjoy the fruit of his labors.

We also see Boaz as a man of wisdom and discretion, proactive and tactful, following through on commitments and always preserving the personhood of those with whom he was dealing.

Finally, we observe him taking upon himself the responsibility of two widows, caring for them, and relating to the one who became his wife in a mature and affectionate manner.

All of this leads us to ask, What lay at the basis of Boaz' well-rounded personality? How had he been able to earn the respect of all in Bethlehem? Why was he able, in each of the scenes described in these chapters, to conduct himself in an admirable manner?

NO SUBSTITUTE

The answer to all these questions seems to lie in Boaz' integrity. He possessed a strong, internal God-consciousness; and in its outworking, the fact that God was a reality to him made a difference in his life.

Consider each of the scenes again:

In Boaz' greeting of the laborers (2:4), he is transparent in his belief that temporal blessings come from God (1:6).

In his concern for Ruth, he is candid as well as concerned

and states his intentions honestly and without ambiguity (2:8, 9).

In the example Boaz set for his servants at lunch time, as well as the instructions he gave them, he demonstrated his integrity. At no time did they receive the subtle message "Do as I say, but not as I do."

In the absence of any feelings of guilt, he and his workers enjoyed the benefit of their efforts on the threshing floor (3:7). He could enjoy the blessings of God's goodness without thinking that such enjoyment was sinful.

In his discernment, he showed his self-control when approached by Ruth (3:9–13), for at this moment she was more vulnerable than she had ever been during the six weeks of harvest. It would have been easy for him to take advantage of her.

In his handling of legal matters at the gate of the city, he preserved the rights of his fellow-kinsman (4:3–10)—all of which was done quite apart from his personal desires.

In his prompt performance of his promise to Ruth (3:13 and 4:13), as well as in raising up a son to the deceased Mahlon (see 4:14–17 where Obed is legally reckoned as Naomi's son), he proved his faithfulness to the revealed will of God.

All of these underscore Boaz' God-consciousness and integrity. The net result was that he enjoyed the trust and respect of all the people.

Furthermore, his integrity enabled him to perceive different issues clearly, equipped him with an independence of thought and action,[5] and preserved him from even the slightest hint of graft or inappropriate behavior.

Such a man can be trusted by his wife, esteemed by his peers, and honored by his employers. He will not need to do things in order to impress people. His chief concern will be to do what is right. This done, all other things will fall into place.

HELP FOR THE UNCOMMITTED

All of this is not without its relevance to us today. The truths from the life of Boaz helped us as we ministered to José. We spent a lot of time with him. Later on, we introduced him to the Bible class. The members, and particularly the men, made him feel welcome. They accepted him. They included him on weekend fishing trips. As they gained his trust, he began to confide in them. He found them to be real people with problems much like his own. No one preached at him or thrust Bible verses under his nose. Instead, privately, they prayed for him.

For about two years, José and Karen attended the Bible studies in the home of our hostess. We could see him struggling with different issues. At different times, each of the men helped him with specific problems. Then one night José wept before the Lord and surrendered his life to Christ.

It was a joy to see him as he began to mature as a Christian and discard his former practices and associates. His macho mannerisms disappeared as he came to understand his new-found identity in Christ. For the first time in his life, he was free to be himself. In addition, his on-the-job performance improved. A new sense of uprightness began to characterize him, and with this came a new confidence. He was becoming a whole person.

José began taking night classes at a local junior college in order to upgrade his marketable skills. In time, he was able to obtain a much better-paying job and make better provisions for Karen and their two daughters.

We wish we could say that Karen also grew through these experiences. We spent time with her, too, showing her how her unrealistic expectations and idealized standards (derived as a child from idolizing her father) were ruining her marriage.

The women in the fellowship also spent time with her, encouraging her and helping her. However, while José grew in his identity as a person, Karen continued in her narcissism (i.e., her love of herself). It soon became apparent that even her daughters had value only as they met her needs.

While it was not easy for José to live with Karen's immaturity, the Lord gave him the grace to persevere. He set his daughters a standard of maturing manhood that they could look up to and admire. However, he avoided the mistake Karen's father had made and readily admitted his failings. He believed that in this way they would not be led to idolize him and thus be tempted to compare their husbands to an unrealistic ideal.

THE PROMISE OF BLESSING

To enjoy fully all that the Bible speaks about when it describes the "rest" of marriage, both spouses must be mature. Boaz and Ruth were.

Furthermore, for marriage to be enjoyable, there must be unity. Apparently Boaz and Ruth were both prepared for Obed to become the adopted son of Naomi and thereby inherit Mahlon's estate. Of course, he would continue in their home and they would rear him, but legally he belonged to Naomi. Such a step involved mutual concurrence. Neither, however, reneged or backed off from their earlier commitment. This showed their integrity as well as their unity. They were both committed to doing what was right.

Interaction

1. Discuss together the five criteria under "Is There an Ideal Kind of Husband?" Consider how well or how poorly

Boaz measures up to your concept of what a husband should be like.

2. Is it possible for a man (or a woman) to be a real Christian in business today? What is required of him (or her)? Describe some of the situations he (or she) is likely to face. Can we learn anything (a) from Boaz' internal God-ward orientation, and (b) his integrity, that will help us face the demands of the present?

3. Assuming that nearly a year had gone by before Obed was born, what reasons might (a) Boaz and (b) Ruth have given for *not* allowing Naomi to legally adopt him? What might they have done? Why? Naomi's adoption of Obed was unopposed by Boaz and Ruth. What does this fact tell you about the kind of relationships they had in their home? How might you have acted in a similar situation?

4. Developing unity in marriage is essential. In Ruth 3:14 we see Ruth and Boaz exercising mutual concern for each other's well-being. In 4:13–17 we see their mutual concurrence in reaching a decision and in acting upon it. How important are these *mutual* processes to the health and happiness of a marriage relationship? What happens when one person makes a decision without consulting the other (Gen. 3:6)? How can true unity be developed?

5. When Boaz took Ruth as his wife it implied an on-going conjugal relationship. Assuming that Boaz and Ruth had other children, how do you think they were reared? What kind of character and evidences of maturity do you think would be reproduced in children with a father such as Boaz and a mother of the caliber of Ruth?

4

A Matter of Priorities

Love like ours can never die.   —Rudyard Kipling

In his poignant description of his courtship of Jean Davis ("Davy" to her friends) entitled *A Severe Mercy*, Dr. Sheldon Vanauken describes how they began working on cultivating unity in their relationship. He and Davy started with a discussion of the things they liked to do most. Then they began sharing in activities they both enjoyed. Their mutual love of beauty, nature, books, poetry, and the freedom of the out-of-doors contributed to their sense of oneness.

Like two streams that run parallel for a time only to merge at last, so the lives of Van and Davy eventually were joined in a loving relationship that was to stand the test of time. As they contemplated marriage, they thought of some of their friends. Loveless unions or broken relationships characterized most of the couples they knew.

Van and Davy traced the origin of the destructive forces in marriage in a "creeping separateness." To protect their union from these same pressures, they erected around their relationship a "shining barrier"—one of total honesty with, and total commitment to, one another. In other words, total sharing. This barrier was to enclose them and preserve their "inloveness" against the corrosive elements of a "creeping separateness" that they had seen destroy other marriages.

The guiding principle of Van and Davy's life together was "The Appeal of Love." Neither would lay down the law to the other. Instead, there would be a frank, loving discussion of all issues. The final appeal always being, *"What is best for our love?"*

The "inloveness" of the Vanaukens was total. It extended to every area of their lives. "The passion, the sexual element, was there [too]: and sexual harmony, like sexual playfulness, was an important dimension of our love. But it wasn't itself the whole thing; and we knew that to make it the whole or even the most important element was to court disaster."[1]

So it was that in one of the greatest true-love stories of all time, the Vanaukens achieved closeness through sharing and kept their "inloveness" growing through all the years of their marriage.

Such closeness is the essence of true union.

IMPORTANT FACTS

In considering the essence of marital unity, we find that the relationship of Hannah and Elkanah illustrates this point as clearly as the lives of Ruth and Boaz portrayed genuine maturity. For a marriage to be successful, according to Genesis 2:24, there must be:

- The development of an authentic maturity;
- The cultivation of a genuine spirit of oneness; and
- The attainment of mutual sexual satisfaction.

Any problems in the relationship can frequently be traced to a failure in one or more of these areas.

A BRIEF REVIEW

Hannah and Elkanah are introduced to us with remarkable economy of words (1 Sam. 1:1–2). They live in a village a few miles north of Jerusalem called Ramathaim ("The Two Ramahs" or "Heights"). In time, this little town would be known simply as Ramah, but at the time of our story it carried the additional descriptive title, "Zophim." Earlier in Israel's history this hilltop village had been established by a man named Zuph, and he had given his name to the entire district (9:5).

Elkanah lives in this town with his wives, Hannah and Peninnah. He is a Levite, of the line of Kohath. His ancestors had originally lived in the territory of Ephraim (Josh. 21:20). From the brief description given of Elkanah, we conclude that he is a man of wealth. He lives on his own property and does not appear to be officiating as a Levite.

Elkanah's first wife, Hannah, had been unable to bear him any children. This meant that upon his death, there would be no one in Israel to bear his name. James Deane, a famous British preacher of a generation past, comments on Hannah's condition:

> [Hannah, whose name means 'Grace'] was a pious, amiable, unselfish woman, one who, in men's judgment, would have been thought a fit person to have brought up children in the nurture and admonition of the Lord; but she had to endure the hard fate of barrenness. What a terrible calamity this was considered by Hebrew women may be gathered from the passionate appeal of Rachel to her husband Jacob: "Give me children, or else I die" (Gen. 30:1). No such impatience was found in Hannah. She is meek and calm even under the grossest provocation. Despairing of offspring from his first

consort, Elkanah takes a second wife, Peninnah, 'Pearl,' or, as we might call her, Margaret, and by her becomes the father of numerous sons and daughters. Vain of her maternity, despising one who was denied the blessing of children, and jealous of the love with which her husband regarded her rival, Peninnah lost no opportunity of deriding and reviling Hannah both in public and in private.[2]

Hannah's husband, Elkanah, impresses us with his spirituality and maturity. He does not take out his disappointment on her. Instead, rising above the common sentiments of his times, he preserves the unity of their relationship by showing her special favor (1 Sam. 1:3–4).

The wisdom of Elkanah's actions may be seen by referring to two passages in the first book of Moses, Genesis 16:3–4 and 29:34. Both deal with the issue of infertility. In the first, Hagar despises Sarah and probably entertains the hope that she will be able to replace her in Abraham's affections. In the second, we see Leah hoping that her numerous sons will displace Rachel and endear her to Jacob. Abraham handled the threat of disunity well.[3] So did Elkanah. He did not permit Peninnah's rivalry to affect his relationship with Hannah.

With this as a brief introduction to the story, let us consider the annual attendance of the family at a festival at Shiloh.

INCREASED VULNERABILITY

Moses had instructed the Israelites that all males were to attend three great religious festivals at the central place of worship. These were the feasts of Unleavened Bread, Harvest, and Ingathering (Ex. 23:14–17).

This rule had fallen into disuse, and by the time of our story, one public attendance each year was thought to be sufficient. For one of these feasts, Elkanah would go up to Shiloh, to the house of the Lord of Hosts, and there worship and offer sacrifices. Women were not required to make this pilgrimage. It is a measure of Elkanah's practical wisdom (in not leaving Peninnah alone with Hannah in the same house) and spiritual zeal that he took his wives and children with him.

Tough Realities

At these feasts, Peninnah would taunt Hannah. Dr. William Blaikie comments on Peninnah's attitude as revealed in 1 Samuel 1:6–7:

> No sense of courtesy restrained Peninnah from expressing her feeling of [contempt for] her rival. No regard for God or His worship kept back the storm of bitterness. With the reckless impetuosity of a bitter heart, she took these opportunities to reproach Hannah with her childless condition. . . . Her very object was to give Hannah pain.
>
> If the heart of Peninnah was actuated by this infernal desire to make her neighbor fret, it need not surprise us that she chose the most solemn season of religious worship to gratify her desire. What could religion be to such a one but a form? What communion could she have, or care to have, with God? How could she realize what she did in disturbing the communion of another heart? If we could suppose her realizing the presence of God, and holding soul-to-soul communion with Him, she would have received such a withering rebuke to her bitter feelings as would have filled her with shame and contrition. But when religious services are a mere form, there is absolutely nothing in them to prevent, at such times, the outbreak of the heart's worst passions.[4]

Such a sowing of the seeds of disunity brought Peninnah no peace; and if her jealousies were in turn transmitted to her children (as they were in the case of Rachel and Leah), then her children would grow to adulthood knowing little of grace and seeking only the gratification of their own selfish desires (Gen. 49).[5]

Natural Reaction

Hannah feels keenly the taunts of Peninnah. She cannot explain her childless state. Her social milieu frowned on barrenness and all sorts of malicious gossip would circulate about those unable to bear children. Evil minds would invent reasons to explain why a sovereign God had chosen to punish with childlessness the past sins of an infertile woman.

Peninnah, of course, as our own story shows, has seized upon the occasion as well as the place to upbraid Hannah. And Hannah, knowing that she is not guilty of the offenses of which she is being maligned, yet unable to answer her rival because of her condition, feels humiliated and oppressed.

It is natural for someone in such an emotional state to become discouraged, despair of help, and finally give way to depression. Hannah, understandably, weeps. It is all she can do. She feels frustrated, belittled, and falsely accused. This, no doubt, pleases Peninnah, for these festivals were supposed to be joyous occasions (Neh. 8:9–12). Peninnah now believes that Hannah is adding to her offenses.

When people are emotionally distraught, they do not feel like being thankful or feasting. Hannah does not. Following the usual sacrifice, Elkanah gives Hannah a portion of the animal he has offered to the Lord. She refuses to join with the family and eat the meal—a meal intended to commemorate God's goodness to them. She does not have a conscious sense of God's blessing. Her emotions, however, are overriding her reason. She feels too upset to join with Peninnah

66

and her children and partake of the food Elkanah has given her.

Elkanah shows us how husbands may handle such situations. He is sensitive to the feelings of his wife. He asks her a question. This has the effect of causing her to think. He then assures her of his love (1 Sam. 1:8). In other words, he takes the necessary action to preserve the unity of their relationship.

Hannah responds positively. We read, "Then Hannah arose *after eating and drinking. . . .*" She responded maturely to Elkanah's words. His questions caused her to think of what her preoccupation with her grief was doing to their relationship. She was then able to handle maturely her grief; and rising superior to the taunts of a jealous Peninnah, she joined with the family in celebrating God's goodness to them.

We should not overlook the fact that in the mature way Hannah handled her emotions, she, too, contributed to the preservation of unity in the home. Had she not done so, she would have placed an additional burden upon Elkanah, for she would have unwittingly put herself in an adversary position to him.

The key to the preservation of unity in a relationship is not to think of ourselves (how *we* feel, what will please *us*, why we want *our* own way), but rather to think and act on the basis of *what is best for our love.*

Groping for Answers

After the meal, Hannah goes into the outer court of the sanctuary. There, with fervency of spirit, she prays to the Lord (1 Sam. 1:9–11). Perhaps she had prayed the same prayer before. This time, however, goaded by Peninnah's taunts, she earnestly entreats the Lord for a son.

Hannah also makes a vow. If God will give her a son, she will "lend him back to the Lord" all the days of his life.[6] He will also be dedicated to the service of God as long as he lives, not merely as a Levite whose duties commenced from his twenty-fifth year and ceased at his fiftieth (Num. 4:3; 8:24–25).

As Hannah is praying, there occurs in verses 12–18 an incident with Eli which shows her ability to cope maturely with the unexpected. Eli interrupts her prayer. Because of the spiritual decadence of the times, he presumes her to be intoxicated. Hannah handles this calloused interruption with dignity and an absence of anger. She respects the office of Eli and responds to him with a quiet, positive statement.

Eli, as God's representative to the people,[7] assures her that her prayers have been heard, and Hannah leaves confident that God will give her a son.

Turning Point

Hannah returns to Elkanah and tells him all that has taken place.[8]

Years earlier, in order to preserve the unity of the home, Moses had included in the statutes that were to govern the lives of God's people a precept that all vows made by women were to be ratified by their husbands (Num. 30:6–15). This was not a restrictive form of legislation. It was instituted to insure that a husband and wife act in concert with one another.

After hearing Eli's words, Hannah fully believes that God has heard her prayer (1 Sam. 1:18). Her faith rises above her circumstances. The question now is, Will Elkanah go along with her vow? Will he permit his son to spend his life serving the priests in Shiloh?

Once again, Elkanah shows his commitment to Hannah. He, too, makes a vow (note 1 Samuel 1:21 and the words,

". . . and pay *his* vow"). The exact nature of his vow is not explained to us. It is possibly one to the effect that, if Hannah does indeed conceive, then he will make a particular sacrifice to the Lord.

Such a spirit of oneness, as is illustrated for us by Hannah and Elkanah, is based upon the mutual respect of a husband and wife for each other. It is not achieved overnight. It requires the steady development of the relationship so that a point is eventually reached where each partner has confidence in the other. When this stage is attained, no aspect of one's life is considered unimportant, and each feels free to share his or her innermost thoughts and longings with the other.

Of course, such self-disclosure involves the element of risk. When we share our innermost thoughts with someone, we become vulnerable. In our story, however, Elkanah gives no evidence of taking advantage of Hannah's transparency. Instead, if we read ahead in the story, after Samuel has been born, we find him encouraging her to confirm her vow to the Lord.

From the example of Hannah and Elkanah, we come to learn that the basis of trust and confidence in marriage must be the sense of "inloveness" that enables a couple to surmount the vicissitudes of life.

A New Perspective

The celebration of the feast being over, Elkanah and his wives and children rise early the next morning, worship before the Lord, and return to their home. This time there are no tears. Hannah believes that Yahweh has heard her prayer (Mark 9:24). Elkanah, too, is resolute in his determination to honor God with a sacrifice, should Hannah indeed conceive.

On returning to their home in Ramah, we read that

Elkanah "knew" his wife. This is a Hebraic expression for sexual relations. The way in which this is mentioned in the text does not imply any special occasion. Rather, it looks at something that took place quite normally.

Some indication of the testing of Hannah's faith may be gleaned from the fact that Samuel was born just before the next annual feast. From this it would seem as if Hannah did not conceive for at least two months. This does not imply disinterest or tardiness on God's part, but rather the process necessary for the maturing of Hannah's faith.

God's promises are sure, but they are not automatic. Sometimes we have to wait for the answers.

In the course of time, however, Hannah finds out that she is indeed pregnant. In her heart she knows that her child will be a boy, and she and Elkanah decide on a name. When she bears him, she calls him *Samuel,* "asked of God."

During the next three years, Hannah devotes herself to rearing Samuel. All that she promised the Lord, she fulfills.

Jewish mothers sometimes suckled their children to the age of three years, and this was probably little Samuel's age when he was taken to Shiloh. Meanwhile, [Hannah] resolved that until that time was reached, she would not go up to the feast. Had she gone before her son was weaned, she must have taken him with her, and brought him away with her, and that would have broken the solemnity of the transaction when at last she should take him for good. . . . The very first visit that she and her son should pay to Shiloh would be the decisive visit. The very first time that she should present herself at that holy place where God had heard her prayer and her vow would be the time when she should fulfill her vow. The first time that she should remind the high priest of their old interview would be when she came to offer to God's perpetual service the answer to her prayer and the fruit of her vow. To miss the feast would be a privation, it might even be a spiritual loss, but she had in her son that which itself was a means of grace to her, and a blessed link to God and heaven; while she remained with him, God would still remain with her; and in prayer for him, and the people whom he might one day influence, her heart might be as much enlarged and warmed as if she were mingling with the thousands of Israel, amid the holy excitement of the great national feast.[9]

A Solemn Responsibility

So Hannah devotes herself to rearing Samuel in Ramah. His physical needs are taken care of as she tenderly watches over him. His mental and emotional needs are met as he comes to realize how special he is. His spiritual needs are also channeled in the right direction as he becomes aware of his dedication to the service of God.

James Deane is convinced that, based upon Elkanah's commitment to Hannah (which prompted him to make a vow) and his subsequent encouragement of her (1 Sam. 1:21–23), he too played an important role in Samuel's early rearing. His role would not have been as active as Hannah's, for infants are more dependent upon their mothers. However, the point that Deane makes is important: "Elkanah did not merely acquiesce to his wife's vow, but he helped her carry it out effectually by his actions and prayers."[10] This reinforced their oneness and prepared Samuel for the future.

KEEPING FAITH

When Samuel is three years old (2 Chron. 31:16), Elkanah and Hannah take him to the sanctuary at Shiloh and there present him to the Lord (1 Sam. 1:24–27). Hannah then reminds Eli of the incident that took place in those same surroundings four years earlier.

We might have expected Hannah to weep on this occasion as well, but for a different reason. Instead of being stricken with sorrow, she rejoices in heart. God has given her the son for whom she had prayed. He had long ago laid claim to the firstborn of every family (Ex. 13:2). Samuel will be safe in *His* keeping.

Once again, Elkanah offers up sacrifices on behalf of his family. A three-year-old bullock is sacrificed as a whole burnt offering for Samuel. He is then brought to Eli.

"And he [Samuel] worshipped the Lord there" (1 Sam. 1:28). There was no separation-anxiety; no sense of being abandoned by his parents, but only a sense of mission. Samuel realized that he had been dedicated to the Lord before his conception. He had imbibed a pious, God-fearing attitude from his parents. He was now ready to spend his life in the service of the One who meant so much to his mother and father.

COMPENSATED

It is significant that Hannah does not ask God for another child. She is content. In His all-wise providence, He has vindicated her from the slander and criticism of those who looked down on her.

God, however, is a God of grace. The next year when Hannah and Elkanah take Samuel a new tunic, Eli blesses them (1 Sam. 2:18–21). The result is that, in time, Hannah bears three additional sons and two daughters. She is more than compensated for the son whom she has "lent" to the Lord all the days of his life.

THE BENEFITS OF ONENESS

Since the publication of *Open Marriage* by Nena and George O'Neill, there has been a strong emphasis on separateness in marriage, that is, an emphasis on achieving one's full potential and on being independent. Slanted phrases like "being hooked on togetherness" and marriage "programming one for dependency," have biased people's minds.

In contrast to this popular trend is the design of God. He never intended marriage to stifle anyone's individuality. Instead, He provided the basis for marriage to be the most rewarding of all of life's relationships.

Unity (or "inloveness" as the Vanaukens called it) needs to be cultivated. It cannot come to full bloom overnight. It does not happen automatically. In the case history of Hannah and Elkanah, we see the reality of their oneness, not the process by which it was achieved. However, the illustration of the harmony they had attained should serve to encourage us. Their oneness helped them withstand pressures from a variety of sources.

The more carefully we probe the biblical text for the source of their intimacy, the more clearly certain principles stand out. We observe the importance of:

- *A total commitment to each other.* Peninnah and all her children could not wean Elkanah away from his love for Hannah; and Hannah shows her commitment to Elkanah by not allowing her emotions to undermine their union (1 Sam. 1:6–9).
- *A total honesty with each other.* Hannah made a vow to the Lord. She then told Elkanah, and he too, made a vow (vv. 11, 21).
- *A total sharing.* Note the openness of their words in verses 8 and 21–23. They were both transparent in their relationship.

The unity of Hannah and Elkanah provided a basis for their worship of the Lord, their home life in Ramah, and the manner in which they reared their children.

- *A total commitment to each other.* Peninnah and all her children could not wean Elkanah away from his love for Hannah; and Hannah shows her commitment to Elkanah by not allowing her emotions to undermine their union (1 Sam. 1:6–9).
- *A total honesty with each other.* Hannah made a vow to the Lord. She then told Elkanah, and he too, made a vow (vv. 11, 21).
- *A total sharing.* Note the openness of their words in verses 8 and 21–23. They were both transparent in their relationship.

The unity of Hannah and Elkanah provided a basis for their worship of the Lord, their home life in Ramah, and the manner in which they reared their children.

Many of the problems afflicting marriages today are caused by disunity, and the damaging effect of a lack of singleness of purpose upon children within the home is plain for all to see.

The time has come for each husband and wife so to commit themselves to each other that they will be able to eradicate any form of "creeping separateness" from their relationship. With this commitment, they will be able to build, instead, a barrier that will preserve their "inloveness."

Interaction

1. As you each reflect upon this chapter, make a list of the pressures, both internal and external, that could have caused a breakdown in the relationship of Hannah and Elkanah. Discuss these together. What did Hannah and Elkanah do to preserve a sense of oneness?

2. The pressure Peninnah brought to bear upon Hannah drove her to prayer. What might Hannah's responses have

been to Peninnah's taunting—verbal rebuttal; endeavoring to draw Elkanah onto her side against Peninnah; the slander of Peninnah for her faults? What does Hannah's response teach us about her person? Is this a good way to handle pressure?

3. Hannah's petition in the sanctuary illustrates the dynamics of effective prayer: (a) Note her *submission* inherent in the word "maidservant"; (b) her *identification* with God and His purpose in the words "LORD of Hosts"; (c) her *fervency* in pleading for God's intervention—something He had promised to do if His people obeyed His covenant (Deut. 7:14); and (d) her *faith* (see 1 Sam. 1:17–18).

Are these four aspects of prayer taught in the New Testament? Where? In what ways may we make our prayer life more effective?

4. How would you describe *transparency* in human relationships? Consider the conversations in First Samuel, chapter 1. What characteristics—honesty, sincerity, being maturely in touch with one's emotions, having the ability to describe one's feelings—do they illustrate? Is the communication of each participant self-centered, defensive, appropriately assertive, supportive, or kind and considerate? How do these elements of communication compare with your usual approach?

5. Problems arise in marriage when a "creeping separateness" is allowed to obscure the primary purpose of the marital relationship. Describe the things in this chapter that could have caused disunity in the relationship of Hannah and Elkanah. Having identified these elements, consider what Hannah and Elkanah did in each instance to preserve their oneness.

5

Differences in Values

*It is not marriage that fails; it is people that
fail. All that marriage does is show
people up.* —Ralph Waldo Emerson

Why do people marry? What causes a man and a woman to
commit themselves, in the presence of God and their assembled friends, to a lifetime of togetherness?

CONFLICTING THEORIES

Psychologists and sociologists have examined the com-
plex issue of mate selection and marriage from every conceivable point of view.

Some researchers such as John Scanzoni in *Social Exchange in Developing Relationships* believe that the basic
quest of individuals is economic security. They are of the
opinion that people marry someone whom they trust will
help them enhance their position socially.

Others such as Robert Winch in *The Modern Family* believe that people marry someone opposite in temperament
to themselves out of a subconscious desire for completeness.

Sigmund Freud, on the other hand, propounded the the-
ory that a young man will invariably marry a young girl who
will grow up to be like his mother, and *vice versa*.

Marriage counselors, depending upon their training, will approach the subject from slightly different points of view. Some will stress the meeting of the material needs as an outgrowth of their system of values, while others may place greater emphasis on the sexual needs of the couple.

For the most part, however, replicated research has tended to show that most men and women marry for companionship (Gen. 2:18). Where this is true, the development of a lasting, satisfying relationship is a distinct possibility.

Not all people marry for companionship, however. Some desire a mate solely to enable them to bear a legitimate child. Then, when this psychological need has been met, they feel that their marriage can be disposed of as easily as a used paper cup from a dispensing machine.[1]

Still others feel that marriage will confer on them some form of adult status. Or they marry because this is what is expected of them. In some areas, for example, executive positions are given only to married men because they are supposed to be more stable.

And, of course, there are those who marry to escape their present situation. They want a home—a place to belong.

Couples who fall into one or another of these categories will need to work hard on building a sense of togetherness. Their experiences to date and the manner in which they have been reared will tend to hinder the development of true unity.

FIRST ACT IN THE DRAMA

The Scriptures illustrate for us a wide variety of marital relationships. Three specific ones concern David. His first wife, Michal, was the younger daughter of King Saul. The other two concern his marriages to Abigail and Bathsheba.

Polygamy was openly practiced in those days, and the number of wives a person had reflected his social standing.

The Setting

Saul had promised his elder daughter, Merab, to whomever killed Goliath (1 Sam. 17:25). The promised bride, however, is never given to David. Instead, he is made commander-in-chief of Saul's army. When not engaged in military campaigns, the young shepherd-turned-soldier plays his harp for Saul in the palace. He is neither hasty in his desire for marriage, nor ignorant of the responsibilities of being the king's son-in-law.

It is probable that during the evenings at court, Michal, Saul's younger daughter, has the opportunity of seeing David as he seeks to quiet Saul's troubled spirit.

Most commentators are convinced that Michal was a precocious young girl of exceptional charm. Dr. Clarence Edward Macartney describes her as the:

> . . . type of a proud and beautiful woman who inspires passionate attachments, and exercises a subduing influence, but being unregenerate and of the world, injures those whom she attracts, and is innocuous only to the lovers who are able to withstand her charms.[2]

A Series of Setbacks

David's military prowess endears him to the people. After a successful encounter against the Philistines, the women welcome the returning warriors with a song. A portion of it runs:

> Saul has slain his thousands,
> And David his ten thousands.
> (1 Sam. 18:7)

Saul is unhappy when he finds himself compared unfavorably to David, his new general. The very next day, he tries to kill him.

Saul's jealousy is such that he does everything he can to get rid of the one whom he has come to regard as his rival. He demotes David and then sends him on dangerous military assignments (18:13). He again offers Merab to David as his wife. At the time of the wedding, however, he gives her to someone else (vv. 17–19). He hopes that this will make David discouraged and either careless or reckless in battle.

Finally, learning of Michal's ill-concealed infatuation for the young commander, Saul promises her to him if he will distinguish himself in battle. David does so and becomes Saul's son-in-law. But the more he prospers, the more bitter becomes Saul's enmity (vv. 20–29).

Short-Lived Happiness

The days of happiness that David and Michal share are few. Jonathan is able to bring about only a temporary cessation to Saul's hostilities (1 Sam. 19:1–7). After David achieves another significant victory over the Philistines, Saul's jealousy causes him to try to kill David once more. The incident occurs after dinner one evening. Saul throws a spear at his son-in-law. David moves quickly out of the way, and it lodges fast in the wall. He then escapes to his home.

There, Michal is either warned of Saul's plans by some servants or sees her father's men in the shadows outside their home. She fears for David's life and persuades him to flee.

With her heart fluttering with nervousness and apprehension, Michal lets David down through a window. Her fears are well founded. But when will she see David again? What will become of her? How will she explain her actions to her father?

As David's feet touch the ground he looks up, she down. Their eyes meet. Love is transmitted from one to the other in that fond farewell. Then turning, David disappears into the darkness.

With David safe, at least for the moment, Michal devises a plan. She takes a statue[3] and a goat-hair pillow and places them in David's bed. Then she waits. Her ruse will be found out sooner or later. She knows this. The important point is for her to give a suitable explanation to her father and stay in his good graces.

By morning, Saul's patience is at an end. He demands that David be brought before him. When he hears that David is sick, he instructs his servants to bring him, bed and all. On entering the home, the soldiers find that Michal has lied to them, and they bring her before Saul (19:11–17).

Again, Michal lies. She claims that David made her make up his bed as though he were in it. And Saul believes her. Apparently anything that points to David's villainy is readily accepted.[4]

But what of her integrity? If she truly loved David, why did she not go into exile with him? And if she chose to stay, was it necessary to lie to her father about David? Michal, it seems, was guided solely by expediency.

Back to Father

Michal apparently goes back to live in her father's court. There palace guards pass on to her maids all the gossip about David. In time, Saul gives her in marriage to Palti (or Paltiel). He loves her, but there is no evidence that she ever returns his love.

If Michal retained sentimental memories of David during

these years, she hid them well. He was an outlaw. Life for her had to go on. Palti's fortunes were not as bright as David's had been, but they were better than waiting for the return of someone who might easily be killed by Saul. She, therefore, made the best of the situation and contented herself with her new relationship.

HARD TIMES AND UNHAPPY CHANGES

The years pass. Perhaps as many as ten in all. Saul becomes involved in a war against the Philistines. He is killed and with him, Jonathon and his other sons.

When David hears this, he inquires of the Lord, "Shall I go up to [live in] one of the cities of Judah?" and Yahweh says to him, "Go up." David then asks, "Where shall I go up?" And the Lord replies, "To Hebron." So David goes to live in Hebron with his two wives, whom he has acquired during his years as an outlaw, and all the men who are with him (2 Sam. 2:1–3).

On hearing that David is residing in Hebron, the leaders of the people of the southern tribes come and anoint him king (v. 4).

David immediately begins to consolidate his little kingdom. Meanwhile Ish-bosheth, Saul's son, is made king over Israel. He reigns for only two years. His general, Abner, becomes impatient with his inept administration and makes overtures to David (3:12ff.). His plan is to unite all of Israel under David's rule. David agrees to meet with Abner, but only if Michal is restored to him (v. 14).

Abner, to advance his own political fortunes, takes Michal from Palti (or Paltiel) and brings her to David in Hebron. And so the pair, who had last seen each other on the night when David fled from Saul, are reunited.

Both Michal and David, however, have changed. Because of the vicissitudes through which he has passed, David has matured. He has grown in his God-consciousness. Michal, too, has changed. Lamentably, her personal pride, vain ambition, and love of prestige have left no room for emotion. She has left Palti to become queen in Hebron. David is no longer a significant entity in her life.

Nora Lofts, in her book *Women in the Old Testament*, comments on the reunion of David and Michal.

> The meeting, after many years, of erstwhile lovers is never an emotionally simple thing. Romantic stories, which pretend that it is so, ignore the work of time and effect to believe that during the interval the minds and bodies of the lovers have been in a kind of cold storage from which at the moment of reunion they are able to emerge unchanged. But the fact is otherwise. Experience develops, and living changes people, and those who come together after years of absence are not identical with those who had parted. So it was with David and Michal. They had both developed along lines which were already laid down for them when they whispered their tearful farewells through the darkness.[5]

Michal had grown hard and conventional. She loved the pomp of the palace and the attention of the courtiers. David, on the other hand, had developed from a talented shepherd boy into a brave, resourceful, and wise king. He also possessed a consciousness of God's eye upon him which motivated all he did. They were reunited, therefore, as total opposites.[6] To Michal, reunion with David meant a step up the social ladder.[7]

GOD'S MAN

The remaining years spent in Hebron see David becoming stronger and stronger, and the northern tribes becoming weaker and weaker. Two of Ish-bosheth's men assassinate him. With no one to lead them, the people of Israel come to David and ask him to be their king (4:1–5:5).

David continues to reign in Hebron until he and his men are able to take the fortress city of Jerusalem. He then makes this city his capital. He also brings up the Ark of the Covenant to Jerusalem with singing and dancing. For the occasion, he lays aside his robes of state and dons instead the ephod of a priest.

At this point we need to reflect for a moment on the office of the priest. The priesthood necessitated that the one officiating so dedicated himself to what he was doing that all selfishness and pride be set aside so that he could truly represent God to the people. "He is self-emptied," wrote Dr. Horton. "The priest's only conceivable attitude is one of indescribable humility; for he is speaking and acting as one in the unveiled presence of God, and in that presence even archangels bow their heads, cover their faces with their wings, and cry 'Unclean.'"[8]

In heading the procession, David first offers up sacrifices. He then leads the people and the priests as they climb the hill toward Jerusalem. The religious enthusiasm of the moment overmasters him. He dances before the Lord. His heart is filled with gratitude to God and the emotion he feels defies more dignified expression.

It is exactly this kind of demonstration of religious zeal that would excite the contempt of Westerners today. We, therefore, must try and look at David's actions as God did. He saw David's heart. He saw that his motives were pure. David was not drawing attention to himself. Rather, he had emptied himself of all that betokened pride and authority, and God accepted his actions as an act of worship.

UNMASKED

God's view of Michal, however, is quite different. Her attitude is laid bare as she watches her husband dancing before the Ark. From her privileged position along the line of the procession, she looks down and sees David, *the king,* dressed only in a plain linen garment. He is also behaving in what to her is an undignified manner. Lacking spiritual sensitivity, she is conscious only of how his actions will reflect on her at court. She feels embarrassed. Her embarrassment, however, soon turns to scorn. The years of growing apart and the incompatibility that she now feels toward all that David represents produce in her a feeling of contempt. She does not wish to be identified with him in his religious zeal, "and she despises him in her heart" (6:16).

David returns to his home happy of heart. It has been a good day. The Ark is now safely housed in Jerusalem. Inwardly, he is rejoicing. His people are happy. God has been honored; what could possibly go wrong?

Michal, however, is waiting for him. As soon as he enters the palace, she pounces on him. Her words are vindictive. She wishes to hurt him.

"How glorious was the king of Israel today, who uncovered himself in the eyes of the handmaidens of his servants as one of the vain fellows uncovereth himself." It was all there—scorn, derision, contempt, and her utter lack of understanding. One can even see the hint that she, the daughter of a king, had a better notion than he, a shepherd-become-king, of how a real monarch should behave.[9] Had David worn his emblems of state and led the procession with pomp and circumstance, Michal would have approved. She may even have joined the procession—provided, of course, she could be suitably attired and display her latest "designer original" dress. But to don a linen ephod and do something for a Someone who is unseen appeared to her to be ludicrous!

"Other men have suffered bitter criticism from their wives and either borne it with fortitude or ignored it. But for David, Michal had trodden on holy ground. His answer to her was simple: 'It was before the Lord which chose me before thy father and before his house to appoint me ruler over Israel.'"[10] Then they parted, each going to his and her part of the palace where, true to nature, they would rethink the affairs of the day and the events that had led up to their brief exchange of words.

There are some who believe that David divorced Michal after this incident. Others believe that "he never looked upon her as his wife again." The text simply reads that she remained childless to "the day of her death" (6:23). It seems preferable to conclude that her barrenness was God's judgment upon her.

COMPLEX ISSUES

In our study of the Bible, we find that people are described as they really were and events as they really happened. The incidents have been recorded so that we may learn from them (Rom. 15:4; note the use of the word *example* in 1 Cor. 10:11). The question before us, therefore, is: What may we learn from this story? Why did Michal's marriage, which began so auspiciously, end so poorly?

There is a verse tucked away in one of Paul's letters that may prove helpful as we consider the marriage of Michal and David. It says simply, "Nevertheless, let each [husband] among you also love his own wife even as himself; and let the wife see to it that she respect her husband" (Eph. 5:33).

David evidently loved Michal. That is why he asked for her to be returned to him as soon as the commander of Israel's army approached him about uniting the kingdom. Michal, however, did not respect David.

In order to learn what we can about the dynamics of unity, we need to consider the teaching of this verse.

Words and Meaning

The word used by Paul to describe the attitude of a wife for her husband is *phobos*. In some contexts it means "fear" (1 Cor. 2:3). In other passages it has the meaning of "reverence" or "awe" (Acts 2:43; 19:17). The object of such "reverential awe" is often God the Father or the Lord Jesus Christ (2 Cor. 7:1; 1 Peter 1:17; 2:17). From the usage of the word, we learn also that we are expected to honor our superiors (Rom. 13:7; 1 Peter 2:18).

The respect a wife should show her husband really stems from her acknowledgment of the position of great responsibility he has been placed in by God. He, therefore, needs her help and support, loyalty and trust.

With these thoughts in mind, let us look again at Michal and apply the teaching of God's Word to her situation.

A Word to the Wise

Dr. Louis Albert Banks observed that:

A woman ought never marry a man she cannot reverence. It is not enough to pity a man's misfortunes or weaknesses and wed him in the hope that you may help him. Such a union brings sorrow and not happiness ninety-nine times out of a hundred. Marrying a man to reform him is directly contrary to the spirit of God's Word. No woman reverences a man who is in need of reformation, and if he will not for love of her, respect for himself, and fear of his God turn from his sins and live righteously before marriage, there is little hope that he will do so afterward. No woman can come to such a wedding with that reverential love and sentiment of honor toward her husband which the Bible teaching requires of a wife.

Such an idea of wifehood, of course, bars utterly marriages of convenience. No woman has the right to marry a man simply because he has money or an acknowledged social position, and because by such a marriage she will be able to escape hard work and wear better clothes and live in more luxurious surroundings than she would without it. Such marriages are plainly immoral. There is no sanctity, no sacredness, about such relations. No woman ever yet truly reverenced her husband who did not love him with all her heart, and, in addition to her love, esteem and respect him, and willingly merge her life into his, acknowledging him as her head and leader, glad and proud to be his companion and helpmeet.

If a wife thus truly reverences her husband, it will be her highest joy to make a home for him which will be worthy of the kind of man whom she has honored with her love and esteem. Her husband will be no more truly the breadwinner than she will be the bread keeper and distributor. She will not regard this as a service any the less honorable than his, though he be governor or president, though he be judge or minister, though he be a great merchant or banker, though he be as famous and popular as an author or an orator, though his name be in all the papers and praised on every lip, and her own personality largely unknown. . . .

The wife who truly reverences her husband will feel that there is no sphere in life nobler than to be the homemaker for her husband.[11]

Focal Point

In addition to this basic attitude, there is also the need for unity in the things one desires. Michal appears to have become possessed with her personal pride and love of prestige. This left no room for others. Her marriage to Palti was one of convenience. When David reclaimed her, she left Palti for the glamour of David's court and the dignity of being queen in his palace.

The challenge facing Michal when she was reunited with David was to identify with him and help him serve his (and her) people. To her, however, the people were merely a means to achieve her personal ends.

Words that Wound

Finally, notice Michal's lack of respect for David. Her words to him when he returned home after bringing the Ark to Jerusalem were laden with sarcasm (1 Sam. 6:20). She had no regard for his person. She wanted only to hurt him.

A wife who truly reverences her husband will find ways to draw matters lovingly to his attention. She will also be supportive of her husband and do all she can to help him. This will contribute to the unity of their relationship.

Let us remember that unity is developed when a couple discusses their differences. They may begin by being far apart. However, as they talk over matters, they are brought closer together. They each have a rationale for their actions. This rationale becomes the basis of their choices. Their choices reflect their inner desires and result in actions. Initially, they may be far apart and quite unaware of how their rational thought processes differ from one another. The impact of their actions may initially trigger a reaction they little expected. However, as they discuss matters together, their thought processes are refined. They are coming closer together. Unity is being developed. And as the process continues, they eventually become of one mind.

Interaction

Samuel Rogers, a nineteenth-century cynic, made the following comment on the seeming universality of incompatibility in marriage: "It doesn't really matter whom you marry, since you're sure to find out the next morning it was someone else."

Cynics always exaggerate the situations they describe. The point of Rogers' observation, however, is that in courtship we put our best foot forward. We try to impress one another favorably. When married, we lay aside the facade and are seen for what we really are.

Unity in marriage may be developed around the following five points:

• Knowing ourselves—our emotional desires, our motivational needs, and the basis upon which we seek to understand and relate to other people. Upon this knowledge of ourselves rests our ability to develop intimacy and closeness.

• Knowing our spouse—his or her personality, beliefs and values, likes and dislikes, needs and aspirations. Upon the accuracy of our understanding of our mate rests our approach to the solving of problems and the resolution of conflict in our marriage.

• Knowing our parents—ours as well as his or hers. The patterns established in their homes and the role models they established will, in large measure, be the basis of our conscious or unconscious behavior and of our husband or wife as well. Upon our conscious awareness of these facts will rest our ability to achieve interpersonal understanding and harmony.

• Knowing our own sexuality—our needs, desires, fears, preferences—from holding hands and cuddling up on the couch while we watch TV to kissing and the more intimate expressions of love. Upon this awareness of ourselves will depend our happiness and our ability to relate meaningfully to our spouse.

• Knowing our respective roles. These change with each couple and also at different times during our lives. We need to be sensitive, therefore, to our particular situation. Upon this knowledge of ourselves will rest our ability to share meaningfully the responsibility of marriage.

Discuss together each of these areas, drawing information as needed from the lives of Michal and David, or your own or someone else's marriage. How may unity in *your* marriage be enhanced through the conscious awareness and practical application of truth from each of these areas?

Differences in Values

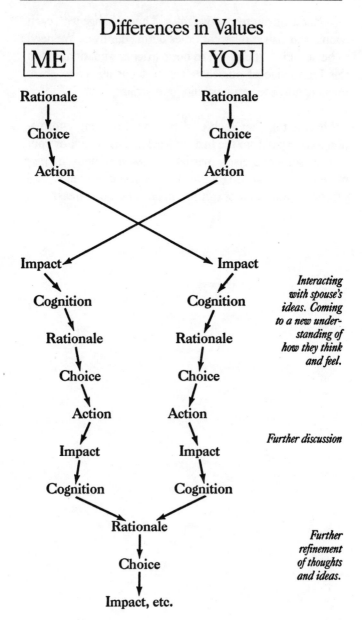

ME   **YOU**

Rationale   Rationale

Choice   Choice

Action   Action

Impact   Impact

Cognition   Cognition

Rationale   Rationale

Choice   Choice

Action   Action

Impact   Impact

Cognition   Cognition

Rationale

Choice

Impact, etc.

Interacting with spouse's ideas. Coming to a new understanding of how they think and feel.

Further discussion

Further refinement of thoughts and ideas.

6

Keeping Things Honest

And on her lover's arm she leant,
And round her waist she felt it fold,
And far across the hills they went
In that new world which is the old.
And o'er the hills and far away
Beyond their utmost purple rim,
Beyond the night, across the day,
Thro' all the world she follow'd him.
—Alfred Tennyson

Why is it that there seem to be so many loveless marriages? We read about them almost daily in the newspaper or in some magazine or other. But more to the point, What can be done to make these relationships better? Does the Bible have any counsel for those involved in this kind of situation?

Jenny had married when she was only eighteen. She had done so to escape an unhappy home life. She was the eldest of seven children. Attractive, yet fearful of men, she had kept house for her father and reared her six brothers following the premature death of her mother. She was often beaten by her father and as often taken into the home of a couple who were members of the church she attended.

Jeff, Jenny's husband, had "swept her off her feet" at an office party. He seemed to offer her everything she had always wanted. They married after only a few months of

93

courtship. Now, with tears running down her cheeks, she was sitting in our living room sobbing out her life's story. The tragedy for Jenny was that after only five years of marriage, Jeff seemed to be becoming a carbon copy of her father.

Quite understandably, Jenny felt trapped.

As we counseled with her, we soon learned that while she would have liked to leave Jeff, she stayed with him, not out of loyalty, but out of fear. She feared being alone. She felt she needed someone, even someone like Jeff. To Jenny, any relationship was preferable to none at all.

A BASIC COMMITMENT

We are in favor of husbands and wives remaining together and working out the problems of their marriage. We rarely have seen a marriage improve where a husband and wife have separated. They may have told themselves that they needed time to think things over, but experience has shown that this seldom works.

We are also committed to helping couples achieve unity and happiness and satisfaction in and from their marriage. But what counsel can be given those who find themselves in a loveless situation?

MEET ABIGAIL

Abigail's name means "my father is glad." It probably signifies her father's happiness at her birth. Normally, men in Old Testament times rejoiced at the birth of their sons. Here, however, we find a father praising God for the safe arrival of a baby daughter. It is possible that Abigail's father already had several sons and that she came along in midlife and gladdened his declining years.

Whatever the circumstances surrounding her birth, we know that Abigail grew up to be an intelligent and beautiful woman. In the record before us, she embodies all of those qualities that men find most desirable in a woman. She is discreet and honest, wise and discerning, sensitive and mature, pro-active and resourceful, brave and kind.

Abigail, however, is married to a man named Nabal. He is described in the Bible as being "very rich . . . [yet] harsh and evil in his [business] dealings" (1 Sam. 25:2–3). His glory is in the abundance of his possessions, and he likes nothing better than to indulge in drunken carousals with those of kindred spirit. Dr. Abraham Kuyper, the famous Dutch theologian-politician, portrays Nabal as "[a man who is] churlishly disposed, and has not a single noble aspiration" in him.[1]

As a couple, therefore, Nabal and Abigail are mismatched.

"How Did I Ever Get into This Mess?"

We should not indict Abigail for marrying Nabal. She was probably forced into the union. Her father may have owed Nabal money, and Abigail may have become the means of the repayment of the debt. Or, if her father were dead, her elder brother may have arranged the match. Nabal was rich. Abigail would, therefore, be well cared for. Furthermore, with his herdsmen taking up more and more of the pasture land, others were being forced out of their ancestral estates. Marriage to Nabal would insure that Abigail would never lack material benefits, and her brothers might be granted certain pastural rights. Whatever the cause, Abigail finds herself in a difficult and trying situation. In spite of her adverse surroundings, she rises above her circumstances and appears on the pages of God's Word as a generous and noble woman. She also stands out as an example of an ideal wife.

Nabal, on the other hand, is possessed of all of those qualities that are unbecoming and repulsive in a man.

CONTRASTS AND CRISIS

In addition to the contrast between Nabal and Abigail, we find in this chapter contrasts between David and Nabal, David and the shearers of Nabal's sheep, and David and Abigail.

David has recently come from one of those mountaintop experiences—those spiritual high points—that make people vulnerable. In 1 Samuel 24, he magnanimously has spared Saul's life. He could easily have killed him. In fact, his men urged him to do so. David, however, is conscious of God's anointing and refrained from following the dictates of his human passions.

As chapter 25 opens, we read of Samuel's death. With this venerated man of God taken from their midst, David fears that nothing will restrain Saul's mad pursuit of him (1 Sam. 25). He, therefore, leaves Engedi and, with his men and their families, moves to the region of Carmel in southern Judah.[2] He takes refuge in the caves near Maon where Nabal's sheep and goat herds graze on the hillsides.

Such is the service that David and his men perform in protecting Nabal's herders from plundering Philistines or wandering Bedouins (1 Sam. 25:16), that no one betrays his whereabouts to King Saul (26:1ff.).

A Time for Festivity

As time passes and Saul seems not to be pursuing him, David becomes more confident. It is springtime and the season for the shearing of sheep. Nabal employs a band of wandering shearers and, after the three-thousandth sheep has been shorn of its wool, they settle down to several days of feasting and debauchery.[3]

David hears of the festivities. He sends some of his men to Nabal with a respectful request that they be given some small compensation for the services they have rendered (1 Sam. 25:6–8). On hearing of David's request, Nabal becomes irate and heaps scorn and ridicule on David and his men (vv. 10–12).

With insult added to injury, and with his dependence upon the Lord not as vital as formerly, David responds to Nabal's words with anger. He is incensed. Controlled when Saul's life was in his hands, David now gives way to a fit of passion. Self-will and the smart of humiliation spur him to action (v. 13). Still giving vent to his feelings,[4] David leads his band of men toward the place where Nabal is entertaining the shearers (vv. 21–22).

Feasting, but With Whom?

The contrast between Nabal's attitude toward David and his obvious rapport with the migrant workers—men described by commentators as shiftless, profligate, and uncouth—should not escape our attention. Furthermore, his lavish entertainment of the shearers and disaffection toward David reveal his real nature. He is callous and devoid of spiritual insight.

His wife, Abigail, however, possesses all the virtues that he lacks. Being spiritually minded, she knows David is destined to replace Saul as king of Israel.

ANGEL OF MERCY

Fortunately for Nabal, one of his young men, having overheard his master speak disrespectfully to David's representatives and knowing that David would not take such effrontery passively, hastily brings word to Abigail. His confidence in her and her ability is most noteworthy. He tells her all that has taken place (25:14–17) and does not hesitate to refer to Nabal as a "worthless man" (lit., a "son of Belial"). Apparently his master's coarse and abrasive manner has alienated even his own servants from him.

No Time to Lose

Abigail immediately sizes up the situation. She is an astute student of human nature. Without a moment's delay, she sets about remedying the wrong done by her husband. The servants respond with alacrity to her instructions. Provisions are hastily laden onto donkeys and sent ahead of her. She hopes these will mollify David's anger and prepare him for what she has to say.

Dr. William G. Blaikie comments on her wisdom and discretion:

> . . . luxury had not impaired the energy of [Abigail's] spirit, and wealth had not destroyed the regularity of her habits. Her promptness and her prudence all must admire, her commissariat skill was wonderful in its way; and the exquisite tact and cleverness with which she showed and checked the intended crime of David—all the while seeming to pay him a compliment—could not have been surpassed.[5]

Apparently, Abigail takes a different route than the one taken by her servants, for she intercepts David and his men before the gifts arrive. The donkeys, laden with provisions, may have arrived as she was pleading with David.

An Impassioned Entreaty

Abigail and David with his four hundred men approach each other quite unaware of each other's presence. They are screened from each other's view by a covert of the hill.

On seeing David, Abigail dismounts and prostrates herself before him. Her thoughts are not of herself. Her entreaty of David is one of the most eloquent in all of Scripture (1 Sam. 25:24–31). To comment upon it would be a great disservice. We will note only a few specifics:

Abigail takes full responsibility for Nabal's offense: "On me alone, my lord, be the blame . . . your maidservant did not see the young men of my lord whom you sent" (vv. 24, 25). Out of *loyalty* to Nabal, she requests that the punishment he so justly deserves fall on her.

Abigail, still prostrate before David, exemplifies true humility. She speaks of herself as David's "maidservant." It is a lowly term for the wife of a very wealthy man to use of herself. There is no pride or haughtiness in her attitude, no bargaining or attempt to buy off David. She may not be able to love and respect Nabal, but she can try to prevent harm coming to him. Her attitude is praiseworthy.

Abigail is also truthful. Her husband's coarse, vulgar ways have become proverbial. She does not try to lie about or to gloss over his reprehensible conduct. Instead, she admits what all know to be true and again tries to divert David's aggression from Nabal to herself.

Abigail is also spiritually insightful. She is convinced of David's destiny. She knows inwardly that the "outlaw" before her will one day become Israel's king. God's anointing rests upon him. She, therefore, reminds him of this and tactfully pleads with him not to do anything now that he may regret later.

Abigail is also generous. She refers to the gift of food she had so hastily prepared (which may have only just arrived), asks for David's forgiveness, and expresses her wish for his future prosperity.

Abigail is also encouraging. She refers obliquely to Saul's

persecution of David and assures him that God will keep him in perfect safety. She also mentions that in God's good time, Saul will be removed from his place with the rapidity and ease with which a stone is slung from a sling.

Finally, Abigail is also reassuring. She closes with a further reference to David's future. She speaks eloquently of the peace he will enjoy because he will not have the gnawing guilt of an accusing conscience and concludes with a request that he remember her.[6] Apparently, her life was far from a happy one!

FEMINISM AND ALL THAT

There are many people today—writers, celebrities, lobbyists, politicians—who believe that the Bible teaches the suppression of women. They are quick to point to a few verses that seem to favor their cause. Unfortunately, they overlook the obvious equality of women so evidently taught in both Testaments.

Abigail's actions in her home on hearing from her servant, as well as her words to David, clearly indicate her independence of thought and deed.

Notice, too, the freedom she feels to reprove as well as to encourage David. The former was done in a spirit of gentleness, while the latter was an outgrowth of her identification with the plan and purpose of God.

The fact that Abigail prostrated herself before David was an act of oriental courtesy. We should not allow this cultural phenomenon to rob us of the beneficial teaching of her example. Nor should we overlook the fact of Abigail's ability. She was able to bring out the best in people. This was certainly true of her servants. They felt a freedom in her presence, and trusted her. It was true, too, of David (note

1 Sam. 25:32–33). Only Nabal seemed beyond her beneficial influence.

With the Bible evidencing so clearly a woman's equality with and influence over man, what more do liberationists want? Instead of attacking the Bible, they should realize that it supports in truth the cause they champion.

THE BIGGEST VICTORY

As we consider further the teaching of this passage, we find that Abigail helps David win his biggest victory—over himself. Notice his response to her tactful remonstrance:

> Blessed be Yahweh God of Israel, who sent you this day to meet me, and blessed be your discernment [of the situation and of what I intended to do], and blessed be you, who have kept me this day from [unnecessary] bloodshed, and from avenging myself with my own hand. (1 Sam. 25:32–33)

Abigail's kind and gracious words convince David that she is genuinely interested in him.

Second, David responds to Abigail's counsel. He cannot refute the wisdom of her words. She has turned his thoughts away from himself and his desires for revenge, to God. As this happened, he has come to realize how wrong his plans have been. He had allowed himself to be ruled by his passions. Her perception of the situation and her gracious way of bringing him to see the reality of what he had planned to do has kept him from shedding innocent blood. David, therefore praises her for her wisdom and discretion.

Third, as we read again verse 25, we see how David assures her that she has made her point. He does not feel humiliated by what she has said to him in the presence of his men. And Abigail does not begin to repeat and reinforce her admonition. Her approach has preserved his dignity as a person. She has left the decision up to him. Her words have merely brought forth the best that is in him.

AN IDEAL WIFE

We cannot leave this section without remarking on Abigail's maturity. We also should note the way in which she did all she could to build unity into her marriage with Nabal.

We find Abigail mature in her person. She is able to administer a large household. She is also capable of mastering her emotions and the personal disappointments of life. She also appears to possess the ability to decide on a course of action, say what needs to be said, and leave others to reach their own decisions.

In addition, we find in Abigail's loyalty to Nabal—loyalty to the point of personal risk—a quality that those in similar situations would do well to emulate.

Whereas many couples continue in an unhappy relationship, each for a variety of reasons, few exhibit the maturity of Abigail or try to maintain unity as she did. Her example, therefore, is laudatory. Only once, at the very end of her impassioned plea, do her emotions rise to the surface and cause her to think of herself (1 Sam. 25:31).

AFTERMATH

Nabal should have counted his blessings in Abigail rather than his sheep. She was worth more to him than all the riches of the kings of his day. Unfortunately for him, he never knew how blest he was!

Ultimate Accountability

Following the meeting with Abigail, David and his men return to their stronghold, and Abigail returns to Nabal's home. He is too preoccupied with his drunken feast for her to speak to him that night. The next morning, however, she tells him everything that had taken place the day before (1 Sam. 25:36–37). Her words are neither spiteful nor vindictive. She does not upbraid him for his conduct. She mentions only what she had done to avoid the slaughter of him and his guests.

In this act, we again see Abigail's tact and discernment. She waits for a propitious time and acts in accordance with her integrity. She does not wait for her activity to be reported to Nabal. Instead, with an inner assurance that she has done what is right, she tells her husband of her actions.

In making known to Nabal what had transpired the day before, we see Abigail's recognition of the headship of her husband. He is God's appointed head over her. Her approach to him, therefore, is that of a person who shares with him the responsibility of the household.

Divine Summons

Nabal is so shocked at Abigail's words that he suffers a paralyzing stroke. Ten days are given him by God to think on eternal realities and repent of his deeds. Then he dies.

Divine Recompense

When David hears that Nabal has died, he thinks immediately of Abigail. Everything about her evokes his admiration. He, therefore, sends a message to her. It is not one of condolence. Rather, it is a message of gratitude and praise. He thanks her for her foresight in restraining him from taking revenge on Nabal, and then asks her to become his wife (1 Sam. 25:39–42). Abigail gladly assents and willingly accompanies David into exile.

The biblical writer then adds this postscript by way of explanation: "For Saul had given Michal his daughter,

David's wife, to Palti . . ." Is the contrast between Michal and Abigail intentional, or are we to see in 1 Samuel 25:42–44 only a cause and effect relationship? Against the latter view is verse 43. Following Michal's marriage to Palti, David had married Ahinoam. It would seem, therefore, as if Abigail and Michal are set in contrast to one another. Michal was self-centered and opportunistic; Abigail was selfless and willing to be supportive of her husband, even if it meant exile.

A MAN'S CHOICE

As we look back over this chapter, we see that David was a man who appreciated the finer qualities of life. He was deeply spiritual himself and he appreciated genuine spirituality in others. It does not surprise us, therefore, that Abigail made a profound impression on him. Their spiritual compatibility gave them a solid foundation upon which to build their relationship.

In the course of time, Abigail conceived. She bore David a son. He was given the name of Chileab (2 Sam. 2:3), meaning "restraint." It was a name derived from David's words in 1 Samuel 25:33, "Blessed be you, who have *kept* me this day. . . ." Chileab was a constant reminder of David's thankfulness for what Abigail had done in restraining him from revenge.

SOLEMN RESPONSIBILITIES

It is tragic to think of a man such as Nabal blighting the life of so gracious and virtuous a woman as Abigail. From his unhappy example of confused values and spiritual insensitivity, we are led to ask the question, "What kind of a man does a woman such as Abigail deserve for a husband? Does the Bible give us a 'blueprint' or model of what husbands should be like?'"

As we think of the self-centeredness, graft, and covetousness of a man such as Nabal, we realize that he exemplifies all the negative traits—what a woman likes least—in the man who becomes her husband. Where, then, do we find an illustration of the positive?

The positive characteristics of a husband are found in Ephesians 5:33, the model of the Lord Jesus Christ and His relationship to the Church.

The Lord Jesus loves the Church and gave Himself for it. The same spirit of self-sacrifice, honesty, and devotion should, therefore, characterize husbands. In other words, Christ becomes *the* model for husbands to emulate, and the Church becomes *the* model for wives to follow.

> The whole philosophy [of marriage] is contained in Ephesians 5:33. The moment we begin to study [it] we find that Paul has here set a great pace for husbands. For we must all admit that the relation of Christ to the church is not that of the arbitrary master or dictator, but that of the most loving helper. Christ, instead of trying to shut us out of equality with Him, gave His life that He might save us from our sins and bring us into an equality with Him, making us fellow-heirs with Him in all the blessings of God. The husband, then, to be properly the head of the wife, must in the highest and noblest sense be her helper and protector. And instead of lording it over her he must seek to bring her into full fellowship with every blessing which he enjoys.

> If we are to follow out this model we shall find some very interesting things for the husband. Christ sets the tone and the spirit for the Church. We are to be like Him. The Church prospers when it is like Jesus. It fails when it falls away from His Spirit. When Christ is present in the Church and the membership associates with Him and loves Him and serves Him with ready minds, then the very atmosphere of heaven

pervades the Church, filling it with peace and inspiring it with courage. Now, the husband cannot escape this great fact, that, in the very nature of things, he makes the tone of the family life. The atmosphere depends very largely upon him; and many a man is complaining of the atmosphere of his home, when he himself is to blame for it. If the husband's habits of thought, of reading, of conversation, are high and elevating, full of intelligence and good cheer and loving sympathy, the wife, and the home itself, will very soon come into harmony with that sort of thing. But if a man's habits are slovenly and neglectful of better things; if he makes of his home only a sleeping barrack and a lunch counter, and confines his conversation to the bare facts of physical existence, which answer to the ordinary grunts or growls of the pig or the dog, in sty or kennel, how can he expect that his wife will maintain against such opposition those intellectual and social and moral habits that will create a home that is full of sympathy and love and intelligence? I repeat it: A husband is the head of the wife in this fact, that he is responsible for the tone of the family life, and nothing can excuse him from it.[7]

He is her protector, helper, inspirer, and supporter. He becomes to her everything she needs. Her responsibility is to respond maturely and positively to his love.

Interaction

1. In considering the sense of unity that Abigail sought to bring to her relationship with Nabal, discuss together (a) what the Bible reveals about him as a businessman and what he was probably like as a husband; and (b) what Abigail was as a wife.

How was she able to retain her integrity and still be loyal to Nabal? What evidence is there in her actions of her commitment to principle rather than a policy of expediency?

2. Consider Proverbs 31:10–31. Without trying to find parallels in Abigail's conduct to each specific mentioned in Proverbs, highlight those verses that find illustration in Abigail's attitude, conduct, or independence of action.

What does this teach us about a wife's ability to do what is right even in the midst of uncongenial circumstances? In what ways did Abigail act in the best interests of her husband?

3. Various women's movements have lampooned the Bible's teaching about women, claiming that it is repressive or illustrative of a culture that finds no parallel in our contemporary society.

(a) Does Abigail fit into the pattern of what liberationists would have us believe? Why?

(b) In this same vein, consider the following quotation taken from John Kitto's *Daily Bible Illustrations:*

> As if to prevent that man should take occasion, from her part in the sad history of the fall, to hold in too light esteem the appointed companion of his life's journey, holding her to be merely a "fair defect of nature," God has chosen to confer singular honors upon woman throughout the sacred Scriptures. They who disparage her capacities, and pour contempt upon her understanding; they who condemn her faithfulness, and distrust her truth; they who make her man's household drudge, or the mere instrument of his pleasures or convenience—have none of them any warrant in Scripture for so doing. . . .
>
> But let us look at the women mentioned in Scripture, and observe how few of them are undistinguished by some useful quality or holy grace. Some are seen to have been endowed before men with supernatural knowledge, being favored by the Spirit of God with the high gifts of prophecy—such were Miriam, Deborah, Huldah, and Anna. Others are noted for

their sagacity and understanding, for which indeed they were proverbial—such as the woman of Tekoah, and the wise woman of Abel-Bethmaacah. Sarah lacked not strong capacities of faith, and strong was the faith of Rahab, of Samson's mother, and of that alien woman whose faith won from Christ a blessing which then belonged to "the lost sheep of the house of Israel" only.[8]

And let us not forget Ruth or Hannah or Abigail. What position is woman really given in the Scriptures?

4. Abigail did not hesitate to speak to David of his intended actions against her husband. She was courteous and appropriately pro-active. What can women learn from her attitude as well as her ability to persuade?

5. Politically, Abigail and Nabal were divided. Nabal followed Saul, the person in power. He spoke scornfully of David. Abigail was more discerning. Discuss the philosophy of each as illustrated in verses 10–11 and 26, 28–31. What does this teach us about each person?

7

Prescription
for Recovery

Age enriches true love. —Gerald Massey

Why did God include the story of David and Bathsheba in the Bible? Dr. Hans W. Hertzberg, a German theologian, has pointed out that the incident recorded in these chapters "has long aroused both dismay and astonishment; dismay that King David, with his manifest piety, could stoop to such an act, and astonishment that the Bible narrates it with such unrelenting openness. . . ."[1]

Does David's affair with Bathsheba encourage moral laxity? Do people feel that, since God did not punish them in accordance with the Law, they, too, may now sin with impunity?

We believe that God included this story in the Bible to illustrate to all succeeding generations mankind's accountability to Him; how He deals with us when we attempt to cover up our sinful actions; and the right way to handle the issues that stem from such deeds.

In addition, and in a more general sense, David and Bathsheba's conduct *after* Nathan's reproof shows us how we may deal maturely with the divisive issues that frequently plague our marriages.

THE ESSENCE OF MATURITY

Maturity is indispensable to marriage. From a human point of view, it involves a process of continuous growth, comprising the following:

• *A realistic view of oneself and others.* This includes an objective evaluation of our strengths and weaknesses, coupled with the ability to understand ourselves and to recognize in our present behavior and reactions the influence of past experiences. This same understanding should characterize our view of the strengths and weaknesses of other people as well.

• *The ability to be accepting of ourselves and others.* This should include the ability to accept ourselves with all of our failings and longings, hopes and fears, personal aspirations and unfulfilled desires. We should accept others with all of their desires and failings, as well.

• *The ability to live in the present* (instead of dwelling on the past or on what might-have-been) *and make plans for the future.* This includes being able to cope with our present circumstances, as well as to make decisions in all areas of our lives.

• *A healthy set of internalized values* (or personal convictions) by means of which we organize and regulate all we say and do.

• *The development of our gifts and abilities* and the utilization of these in creative, reality-oriented ways.

A CASE STUDY

The story of David and Bathsheba serves to illustrate the way in which a couple may realistically and responsibly acknowledge their shortcomings and work toward establishing maturity as well as unity in their relationship. As Dr. Raphael Patai observes, "in the case of David and Bathsheba, sexual desire flared up at first sight but [later] matured into love."[2]

Sin's Course

The story is told with such brevity that our tendency is to read it without being aware of all of the facts (see 2 Sam. 11:1–5). In addition, we need to disabuse our minds of much of what we have read or heard. David, for example, is often indicted because (as is popularly claimed) he was in Jerusalem when he should have been in the field of battle leading his men.

Upon more mature reflection, it appears as if, with an expanding kingdom to maintain, David and Joab shared the command of the army. Joab would lead the army of Israel when affairs of state required David's presence in Jerusalem, as for example in 2 Samuel 10:7–14 and 11:1 with 8:1, 3–8, 15 and 10:17ff.

If this is the case, then it underscores the fact that, as with David, we are liable to temptation when we are engaged in that which is perfectly legitimate.

For us to understand properly what God's Word reveals, we should also note the passage of time between 2 Samuel 11:1 and 2, 4, and 5, and the fact that Nathan came to reprove David for his sin after Bathsheba's baby had been born (2 Sam. 12:14).

The Vulnerability Factor

As we examine the story, we find that the seige of Rabbah is taking longer than expected. Spring has turned into summer. The heat of the day forces the residents of Jerusalem to take an afternoon siesta.

David's palace, having been built on the ridge of Ophel, benefits from any cool breeze that blows across the valley. A summer house has been erected on the roof, furnished with a couch and possibly some rugs and cushions. There, David can play his harp and commune with the Lord. There, too, when it is not too hot, his counselors can recline on the cushions and rugs and discuss with him the affairs of his expanding empire.

David's palace looks down on the flat roofs of the homes of many of his subjects. Their houses have been built on the sloping hill leading down to the Kidron Valley.

One day, toward evening, David rises from his couch and looks out over the city. Some of the houses still shimmer in the heat. But there, in a secluded section, he sees a woman bathing herself (Lev. 15:19; 2 Sam. 11:4). He is fascinated. She is very beautiful and he continues watching her. Lust is conceived in his heart. The more he watches, the more he wants her.

David makes suitable inquiries and learns that she is the granddaughter of Ahithophel, his wisest counselor, and the daughter of Eliam, his trusted friend (2 Sam. 15:12; 23:34). She is also married to Uriah, one of his most loyal warriors (23:39).

None of these considerations deter David from his adulterous desires, and he invites Bathsheba to the palace. There, he seduces her.

Important Motives

But why did Bathsheba bathe herself on the roof of her house and expose herself to the possibility of someone seeing her?

In probing for the reason behind her action, we can begin from the premise that Bathsheba possessed the normal sexual needs of a healthy woman. Her husband has been away fighting with the armies of Israel for about three months. Her unfulfilled sexual desires may now have subconsciously prompted her to do something daring.

In addition, it is not beyond the realm of probability that, if her home stood close to the wall of the palace, it was on a slight elevation to the other houses. With all of Jerusalem taking a siesta and with the parapet of her house screening her from the view of all below her, to bathe unseen on the roof of her home was a tempting prospect. It would certainly be much cooler than bathing indoors.

It may have been, therefore, that with a combination of unmet needs and readily conceived assumptions, Bathsheba engaged in her memorable purification rites. Her repressed desire for sexual expression may have been subtly expressed through her behavior without her being consciously aware of it.

If this is so, then it further illustrates our vulnerability and the need for us to be maturely in touch with our feelings. Only as we are able to monitor our feelings will we be able to avoid being drawn into unwise situations.

Issues and Explanations

As we study the passage further, certain questions concern us. For example, on being invited to the palace, did Bathsheba protest David's advances as Tamar would later do (2 Sam. 13:11–14)? Did she remind him of his loyalty to his friends? Did she call loudly for help (Deut. 22:23–26), plead her marriage vows, and desire to remain faithful to Uriah?

The Bible gives no evidence of any attempted resistance on Bathsheba's part. David, it seems, did not have to coerce her (2 Sam. 13:14 KJV).

It is true that, in the Near East, the kings of pagan countries stood above the law. They could do as they pleased. In

Israel, however, God was the supreme Judge of His people, and no one could sin with impunity (Deut. 22:22). Being knowledgeable of God's law, both David and Bathsheba knew they were doing wrong.

Results

Following the night spent in David's room at the palace, Bathsheba returns to her home. With her sexual desires satisfied, she now experiences feelings of guilt. These feelings are probably heightened by her sense of having betrayed Uriah's confidence in her. She may also have experienced a tinge of fear: having just finished menstruation,[3] would she now become pregnant?

A month passes. Bathsheba's anxieties have now increased. While at first she hoped she would not conceive, now she knows beyond all doubt that she is pregnant. She sends a brief message to David: "I am with child." It is a plea for help that cloaks her mounting desperations.

To cover their adulterous affair, David has Uriah recalled from the field of battle (2 Sam. 11:6–13). He entertains him and then recommends that he take some well-deserved rest and recuperation. Uriah, however, refuses. He chooses instead to sleep with David's servants in the palace.

David's conduct now follows the typical pattern of one who is trying to repress his feelings of guilt. Having tried unsuccessfully to cover his sin by suggesting that Uriah go home to Bathsheba and "wash his feet,"[4] he now becomes desperate. He, therefore, begins to plot the murder of his friend. To accomplish this, he will need an accomplice. He, therefore, sends a message to Joab (2 Sam. 11:14–15), outlining a plan whereby Uriah can be killed.

Cover Up

David's plan succeeds. Uriah dies at the hands of Ammonite bowmen (11:18–25). There is now no one to point an accusing finger at him.

Does Bathsheba surmise that Uriah's death is on her account? All we know is that she mourns for him in the traditional manner. Then, at the end of the week, David sends for her and takes her as his wife.

The official explanation is probably to the effect that the king had promised Uriah he would care for Bathsheba should anything happen to him.

Such perfidy, however, is unbecoming a man of God, and the inspired chronicler adds, "But the thing that David had done was evil in the sight of the LORD."

Sins of the Past

As time passes, it seems as if David's strategy has worked. Bathsheba's child is born and is probably regarded as premature. He is a delight to both his parents and they love him dearly. Their sin, it seems, has been successfully concealed.

The months given David by God in which to repent have been spent, instead, in repressing his feelings of guilt (Ps. 32:3–4). God now sends Nathan to him. The prophet tells the king a story that arouses David's ire (2 Sam. 12:1–6), and he pronounces sentence upon the offender. He little realizes that he is the object of Nathan's parable.

Only when Nathan's accusing finger points at him, does David repent (2 Sam. 12:7–13; Ps. 32, 51). His sin is pardoned, but as a penalty, the child is to die. Furthermore, the sins that he has committed are to recur in his family for years to come.

WEAKENED LEADERSHIP

From this time onward, David's ability to govern his people is impaired. Dr. John Kitto has noted *three* areas in which David's life and service to the nation show the effects of his sin with Bathsheba:

1. *David's ability to execute justice with equity declined.*

Following the exposure of his adulterous affair with Bathsheba and his murder of Uriah, David's subjects must have noted a reluctance on the part of the king to punish offenders in accordance with the law. Men such as Joab and Shimei, Ammon and Absalom sinned with impunity.

In addition, David's perception of certain situations was impaired (as in the case of Ziba, 2 Samuel 16). He now seemed to lack the confidence that formerly he possessed.

2. *David's authority in his own household dwindled.*

He now became overindulgent as a parent. In time, his own sons would openly reject his headship. First Absalom and then Adonijah would try to wrest the kingdom from him.

3. *David's former exuberance and enthusiasm disappeared.*

He became more passive (or permissive), more humble, contrite, and patient. But with the waning of his impulsivity, he also lost a dynamic quality of his leadership (1 Kings 2:5–9). The price of his sins, therefore, was high![5]

TURNING FAILURE AROUND

While we may not fall prey to the precise sins of David and Bathsheba, situations do arise in our marital relationships that impair our ability to function effectively. When this is coupled with a diet of relativism in ethics and of pleasure-seeking as the goal of life, the net result is that devotion to our spouse is replaced by an emphasis on our personal needs.

The irony of our contemporary situation is that, while many alluring prospects of happiness are offered us, marriage as described in the Bible—God-centered and other-directed—still offers the greatest potential for real happiness, contentment, and growth. It is also more preferable than any of the alternatives presently available.

Marital *happiness*, however, is for those who are mature, for those who have

- A realistic view of themselves and their spouse;
- An acceptance of themselves and their spouse;
- An ability to live together with an emphasis on present realities, while also planning for the future;
- A well-developed system of values; and
- An ability to cope with the task of living, while continuing to grow as persons.

These criteria are far-reaching in their scope. They also are of vital importance to each one of us, and their development will help guide the course of our lives. In the next few pages, we will apply these essentials of maturity to the situation of David and Bathsheba.

The Source of Trouble

For David and Bathsheba, the source of their trouble lay in their unconfessed sin. A full year passed before Nathan confronted David with the evidence of his perfidy. During that year, David did not have a realistic view of himself. He tried instead to repress all thought of his actions.

When David's shameful deeds were exposed by Nathan, his immediate response was one of confession (2 Sam. 12:13). His psalms show that he came to a mature assessment of himself before the Lord (Ps. 32:3–5; 51:3).

It would appear as if Bathsheba also repented of her actions when her child became ill, for she was later able to relate meaningfully to David and receive tokens of God's grace (2 Sam. 12:24). She would not have been able to do this, had she not come to a mature realization of herself and of her sin and recognized the same humanness in others.

This kind of honest assessment of oneself is essential if we are to attain to any degree of personal maturity. We must also be free from the tendency to attach to anyone else blame for the actions we have committed. Then, as we see ourselves as we really are, we can respond to situations in our lives with better discernment.

Turning Point

Upon an awareness of ourselves as persons—our strengths and weaknesses, our gifts and limitations—depends our acceptance of ourselves as we really are. This begins with a conscious awareness of our acceptance by God (Ps. 32:1–2; 51:1–3, 5–6). From this premise, we can accept ourselves as He accepts us. With past sins forgiven and blotted out, we can then begin to enjoy new confidence in our standing before him. And from this position—which is all of grace, Romans 5:2—we can accept others with all of their imperfections.

There is great freedom in this kind of mature acceptance of ourselves and of one another. We no longer have to wear masks or pretend to be what we are not. Instead, we can be transparent before each other. This is essential to our maturity as individuals and to our growth as a couple.

A New Realism

Building upon a mature assessment of ourselves and an ability to accept ourselves with all of our limitations is our ability to live in the present and make plans for the future. We no longer need to be shackled to the past by guilt or an accusing conscience.

Notice how this is illustrated for us in 2 Samuel

12:15–23. David did not dwell on the past. He acknowledged his sin. Then he devoted himself to the needs of the present. He prayed for a whole week for his son.

When his son died, David washed and anointed himself, and went into the house of the Lord and worshiped. He did not grieve over what could not be altered. When questioned about his conduct, he expressed his confidence of one day being reunited with his son (2 Sam. 12:23). In this way, he showed his hope for the future.

But notice, too, verse 24. It contains another illustration of David's ability to live in the present. He did not forget Bathsheba. Their marriage may have had a bad start, but the sincerity of their confession and their mature acceptance of each other paved the way for the development of their relationship.

David went to comfort Bathsheba. She received him without spiteful words or recrimination. Such was the extent of their growing maturity that they ended the night by sharing intimately with each other. She conceived, and the inspired penman writes that she "gave birth to a son, and [David] named him Solomon [meaning 'peaceful']. And Yahweh loved him." The months of unrest during which they tried to repress their sin were now over. God was at work in their lives. The birth of a second son was seen as God's compensation for the son they had lost. In naming him Solomon (from *shalom*, "peace"), David was again looking to the future and anticipating the blessing of God upon his son's life and the peace that would characterize his reign.

Needed: Principles

Through their experiences, David and Bathsheba came to embrace an internalized system of values. Notice what God said to David in Psalm 38:8–9 and David's response in verses 10–11.

Values are not rules. Rules frequently degenerate into legalistic prescriptions that lack vitality. Values are principles that we have tested and approved (Ps. 51:6ff.).

David's new sense of values may also be seen by reflecting upon Psalm 51:7–17. He now prized truth and purity, joy and gladness of heart, steadfastness of purpose and fellowship with the Lord. These were deemed to be more important than all the temporal blessings accumulated during his reign. And being teachable, he was now in a position to teach others (v. 13). This involved being open, honest, and transparent before those whom he wished to instruct.

Private Life, Public Policy

Had David not committed adultery with Bathsheba, he would have ruled his country and his family with strength and confidence. Although he lived for another twenty years, the biblical text records him enduring continued opposition from within his own family (2 Sam. 16–18), from Sheba the Benjamite (2 Sam. 20), and from the Philistines (see 2 Sam. 21:15ff.; 21:18ff.).

There can be no doubt but that David felt his hand weakened as a result of the sins he had committed. His subjects were also probably less inclined to trust him. He had mortgaged their confidence. The important point to notice is that, following his repentance, God did bless him (1 Chron. 29:28). In spite of his sin, David was regarded by later generations as Israel's ideal king. He serves, therefore, as a lesson to us of the way in which sin operates in our lives to bring about our downfall; the manner in which we may be reinstated in God's favor through confession and repentance; and the way in which we may maturely handle failure.

Regardless of the occasion of failure in a marriage, the path of recovery invariably involves the five aspects of maturity mentioned in this chapter. If David and Bathsheba found that they worked, so may we.

Interaction

1. Maturity needs to pervade every area of our lives. Discuss the ways in which a husband and wife may (1) have a realistic view of themselves as well as of their mate (with an appropriate balance where their strengths and weaknesses are concerned); (2) be accepting of themselves and each other, with due recognition of the subtleties of perfectionism and of unrealized expectations; (3) assess the truth about their present situation and plan realistically for the future; (4) share meaningfully with each other regarding their values and what they feel is important; and (5) plan now how they are to develop their abilities and broaden the sphere of their interests.

2. Go over the story of David and Bathsheba and pinpoint the tensions for Bathsheba caused by her disloyalty to Uriah. Consider, too, her marriage to Uriah from God's point of view (for she is continuously referred to as Uriah's wife until *after* her child dies. 2 Sam. 11:26; 12:10, 15, 24).

Discuss the ways in which David brought unity into their relationship after he had married her (consider also his protection of her, 2 Sam. 11:27; his kindness toward her, 2 Sam. 12:24; and her apparent ease in his presence, see 1 Kings 1:15–21, 28–31). What do these teach us about their relationship?

3. Reflect on the grace of God in forgiving David and Bathsheba's sin (see Deut. 22:22; 2 Sam. 13:13; Ps. 51:1–4, 7, 10). Did the Mosaic law prescribe any sacrifices

for the expiation of the sins of adultery and/or murder? What does this teach us about God's grace?

4. Dr. Clarence Edward Macartney has observed that while the sin of David and Bathsheba was forgiven, its penalty was not remitted (2 Sam. 12:7–14). How does this relate to the view of those who think that they may sin with impunity? In what ways are the effects of our sins visited upon us—through family, friends, work, etc?

5. The sins of Christians give non-Christians occasion to revile God (12:14). How? What can a believer do to prevent this from happening?

Should we unwittingly give other people cause to reproach God on account of our failure, what should we do to correct the false impression we have created (Ps. 51)? What process had taken place in David's heart that finally enabled him to become a teacher of others?

8

Key to Success

*Nothing is better than a well-dispositioned
wife.* —Albertano of Brescia

What do you want most from marriage? How would you describe your deepest desires? After you have eliminated all the superficial things that you allow to clutter up your life and relationships, what do you believe you need to make your life truly happy?

RESTORING THE FOCUS

In his bestseller *Sayonara*, Pulitzer Prize-winner James Michener contrasts Western marriages with those of the Orient. His story is set against the background of the Korean War and deals with the reasons why large numbers of American servicemen chose to marry Japanese women.

Among these men is a hot-tempered Irishman named Joe Kelly. Joe falls in love with Katsumi, a big round-faced girl with prominent cheeks, oil-black hair, and a gold front tooth that catches everyone's eye when she smiles. By his own admission, however, Kelly feels that his bride-to-be will fill his heart for the rest of his life.

The central figure in the story is Major Lloyd Gruver, an Air Force ace engaged to a girl named Eileen, the daughter of his superior officer, General Webster.

Through a series of encounters, Gruver is given good cause to ponder American-style marriages. The first of these comes from a conversation with Joe Kelly. Joe remarks:

"You ever been in the bunks at night? Men with wives back in the States talk about Junior's braces and country club dances and what kind of car their wife bought. But men with Japanese wives tell you one thing only. What wonderful wives they have. They're in love. It's that simple."[1]

Later on, after being reunited with Eileen, Lloyd begins having second thoughts about marriage. Eileen's ideas and ideals seem to be focused on externals. He feels that he will merely be the means whereby she accomplishes her ends.

The more Lloyd and Eileen are together, the more he detects in her a subtle tendency toward being domineering. The break in their relationship comes when he finds her using *love*—her "love" for him and his "love" for her—as a manipulative device to coax him into fulfilling her desires.

The contrast between Joe Kelly's happiness and Lloyd's unhappiness is heightened at Joe's wedding. Lloyd talks briefly with the American Consul's assistant who will be one of the witnesses. They are alone in the office. He asks her why so many Americans seem to prefer Japanese women.

"They make their men feel important," is her startling and insightful reply. Then she continues, "I try to build my husband up—as a wife should. But with me it's a game. With these ugly little round-faced girls it isn't a game. It's life."[2]

As Michener's story continues to unfold, the reader is brought to see clearly the selfishness of many modern American marriages. Instead of being partners in a mutually satisfying relationship, each spouse leads a separate life and is intent on fulfilling his or her desires. Then, with compromises here and there, each endeavors to use the other to get what he or she wants.

Lloyd Gruver's reflection on the sterility of such unions, as well as the obsessive quest for status symbols and other externals, leads him to take a closer look at the attitude of married Japanese women. They appear happy and content. Their joy comes from within and is expressed through their relationships with their husbands.

Sayonara is indeed a "farewell." In the end, Lloyd Gruver returns to the United States. The way the story concludes leaves the reader with the painful impression that he has left the best behind him for a conventional marriage to Eileen.

USES OF THE PAST

Before we dismiss with a wave of the hand what James Michener has written, let us consider the wisdom that comes from another source, the Bible. In its pages we read of Esther, a Jewish girl who became the queen of Ahasuerus, king of Persia. Every reference to her indicates that she possessed the ability to meet her husband's needs and to make him happy.

Meet the Groom

King Ahasuerus of the biblical record has been identified as Xerxes (486–465 B.C.) of secular history. He ruled over Media and his empire extended from the Indus River to the Mediterranean, from the Bosphorus to Ethiopia.

The Greek historian Herodotus describes in detail the exploits of Xerxes' father Darius the Great and the ambition of his mother Atossa, daughter of Cyrus the Great and sister of Cambyses. In his youth, Xerxes lacked nothing and was daily trained in violence and the despotic satisfaction of his desires.

Soon after the death of his father, Xerxes puts down revolts in Egypt and Babylon, exacting harsh penalties of the offenders. He then undertook the conquest of Greece. To do this, he summoned to Susa all the satraps from the 127 provinces of his realm (Est. 1) and outlined to them his plan. He then sent them back to their provinces to raise his army by whatever means they chose.

Xerxes' invasion of Greece was beset by problems. He was emotionally distraught over the deposition of Vashti (vv. 1:9–22). The first bridge built across the Hellespont was destroyed in a storm. Xerxes was so irate that he commanded the waters of the ocean (representing the back of the sea god Poseidon) to be scourged. He also had chains thrown into the sea to bind the sea god so that he would not be able to destroy the next bridge he wanted built.

Other evidences of Xerxes' impulsivity abound. For example, when his vast fleet was destroyed in the battle of Salamis, he ordered the admiral executed. His harsh, authoritarian manner caused the desertion of his naval forces; and in the battle of Peataea, a large portion of his army left him and joined the Athenians against him.

Finally, Xerxes was compelled to return to Susa and content himself with ruling over the 127 provinces of his empire. What is revealed about him by secular historians serves to highlight the character of the man whom Esther was compelled to marry—a man who had impossible standards of attainment set for him by his parents, believed himself to be all-powerful (but who was in reality weak and insecure), relied heavily upon his counselors, was given to rash judgments, had no respect for human life, and was harsh and unreasonable in his dealings with others.

Here Comes the Bride

What kind of wife does a man such as Xerxes choose? Someone like his mother to dominate him? A sex symbol to be at his beck-and-call? Or a doormat to be used, abused, and then discarded?

Following his humiliation at the hands of the Greeks, Xerxes returns to Susa. He longs for Vashti. His counselors see this and suggest a plan that they feel sure will please his vanity:

> Let beautiful young virgins be sought for the king, and let the king appoint overseers in all the provinces of his kingdom that they may gather every beautiful young virgin to Susa, the capital. . . . Then let the young lady who pleases the king be queen in place of Vashti. (Est. 2:2–4)

Their suggestion pleases the king, and he does accordingly.

Esther, the woman whom Xerxes chooses to be his new queen, has several strikes against her:

She is an orphan. Her parents have died, and she has been reared by her cousin, Mordecai, who is much older than she (2:7).

She is very beautiful, and at this particular time, beauty is a decided liability. She is taken into the king's harem and, but for the providence of God, may never know the joys of having a husband or a family of her own (2:8, 12–14).

She is a Jewess—a member of a despised and troublesome race (2:10; see also Ezra 4:7–22)—who has been born in the land of her captivity.

She is also young—probably no more than fourteen or fifteen years old at the time of our story—a virgin, and sexually inexperienced.

If chosen to be Xerxes' new queen, she will become his second wife and succeed Vashti, whom he still misses.

And if these are not obstacles enough, the statistical improbability of Esther winning Xerxes' favor is about one in 360.[3]

THE BEAUTY CONTEST

Beauty contests are not the smiles and laughter, tears of happiness and stories of success that we imagine them to be from watching television. Behind the scenes, the competition is vicious. Only one will be crowned queen, and each contestant is intent on putting down her rivals in order to advance herself.

The competition in which Esther is engaged is far more serious. The stakes are higher (Est. 2:14), and the future happiness of each contestant depends upon her performance.

Esther possesses the ability to impress people. When given into the custody of the chief eunuch, she "pleases him and finds favor with him" (v. 9). Hers is a quiet, unobtrusive confidence, an assurance that no matter what the outcome of the contest may be, she will find contentment in being herself. This inner calm frees her from anxiety and enables her to be pleasant and cheerful and to take an interest in others.

Esther's inner beauty—that which causes other people to take an instant liking to her—reflects the way in which she has been reared by Mordecai. He has loved her as his own daughter (2:7). He has given her positive assurances of his acceptance of her. He has also set for her a positive example of true manhood. She has learned to relate to men by relating positively to him. As a result, she has grown up feeling respected, valued, and confident. This has equipped her with the ability to be responsive (as opposed to self-seeking) and sensitive to the needs of others.

The Procedure

Following a full year of purification (2:12), during which the young women are also given sexual instruction,[4] each contestant spends a night with the king.

Before going to Xerxes' apartment, anything she desires by way of cosmetics, apparel, or jewelry is given her. These will be the only possessions she will take to the second harem the next morning (vv. 13–14). She will not again spend a night with the king unless he delights in her and asks for her by name.

The Decision

In the tenth month, Esther is finally slated to ascend Xerxes' couch. She does not request anything for herself except what the king's eunuch advises (2:15). Then, knowing how important this one night is, she walks across the courtyard with Hegai to Xerxes' rooms.

What happens behind the closed doors and silken drapes of Xerxes' suite is unknown. We do know, however, that when those doors open again, it is to announce that the contest is over. Xerxes has found the one who is to replace Vashti. It is also noteworthy to read that Xerxes "loved Esther more than all the women, and she found favor and kindness with him more than all the virgins, so that he set the royal crown on her head and made her queen instead of Vashti" (v. 17).

Xerxes then gives a party, a big feast, at which he officially presents Esther to his court as his new queen.

The Reason

But why did Esther "find favor and kindness" with Xerxes? Was it because she was more beautiful or had greater expertise as a lover? Plainly, no. Was it because she was more witty or a better conversationalist? Again, no.

The reason for Esther's success seems to lie in the fact that she had the ability to promote an affirming experience for Xerxes. She respected his person, but not with a fawning humility that masks ulterior motives. She knew how to make him feel secure in her presence. She made it easy for him to be himself. He did not feel threatened. The "little boy" that was in him, that was always struggling to be what his parents wanted, was suddenly able to be himself. In Esther, he had found someone who would not betray him, exploit him, or emasculate him. She was what he had always wanted. And with boyish impulsivity, he stopped the contest and made Esther his new bride and queen.

NOT ALL SUNSHINE AND ROSES

The story of Esther has been retold with great skill by many different writers. We will not dwell on all the details that have surfaced as a result of their arduous studies. Instead, we will concentrate our attention on the relationship between Xerxes and Esther.

Xerxes did not suddenly become mature when he married the young girl who now sat by his side on the throne. He remained weak and insecure, impulsive and forgetful (Est. 2:19–23; 4:8–10; 6:1–9). Though he loved and respected her, there were times when he behaved more like an irresponsible adolescent than a mature man. His immaturity would sometimes erupt in a macho expression of aggressiveness with a corresponding desire to dominate others. This was invariably acted out toward one or more of those in his harem, with the result that he tended to neglect Esther.

The biblical text confirms this by recording that, on one occasion, for an entire month Xerxes preferred others from his harem without once inviting Esther to visit him (Est. 4:11). The reason is not given, but his conduct does point to his inability to relate consistently on a mature level to someone such as Esther.

When Esther does enter the king's judgment hall, we see again her immediate influence on him (5:1–4). We should also note that no word of rebuke falls from her lips for his neglect of her. Furthermore, at no time does she place him in the position of a "little boy" being scolded by his "mother." Instead, she affirms his sovereignty and is respectful in stating her request.

When Xerxes joins Esther for dinner, her sensitivity to the situation leads her to believe that the time is not right for her to place before him her petition. She, therefore, requests that he dine with her the next day also (5:7–8).

During the night, Xerxes suffers from insomnia. He has his chroniclers read to him of his accomplishments. He hopes, thereby, to be able to fall asleep. Morning, however, finds him still awake. He, therefore, rises and with Haman his counselor, again visits Esther.

This time, in answer to Xerxes' request, Esther shares with him the reason for her invitation (7:3–6). Her words are plain and to the point. She knows when to speak and when to stop. There is in her statement an absence of recrimination and no repetition of her point once it has been made. Her attitude and approach recognize Xerxes' authority. At no time does she try to manipulate him into doing what she desires. Instead, there is evident in her words a loving, stable, transparent personality.

Xerxes trusts her implicitly. He gives judgment upon Haman without asking for any corroboration (7:8–10). He then permits Mordecai to issue a decree making the former one by Haman of little effect.

SEPARATE BUT EQUAL

There are many practical lessons to be gleaned from a study of the relationship of Xerxes and Esther. The question of paramount importance to us is, To what may we attribute Esther's success as the wife of Xerxes? Why was she able to exert such a profound influence upon him? What caused him to love her more than anyone else?

The secret is not hard to find. It is found in the way real, genuine love expresses itself.

First, *Esther accepted Xerxes as he was.* She did not try to change him. She did not try to make him more like Mordecai and thereby fit her idea of what an ideal husband should be like. She accepted him as he was, without any reservations or provisos.

Second, *in their relationship there was an absence of competition.* Xerxes felt relaxed in Esther's presence. Each treated the other as an equal. Xerxes knew he could trust her. In fact, from the evidence before us, he had such implicit confidence in her that he never questioned her judgment (7:5–7).

Third, *on Esther's part, there was an absence of self-seeking.* She did not need things to enhance her sense of worth. Xerxes spent his life in an atmosphere of political graft, power struggles, and corruption. It was a pleasant change for him to be in Esther's company. She did not want things; all she wanted was to make him happy.

Between the Lines

As we further consider the information before us, we find that the backgrounds of Xerxes and Esther—which were radically different—had a profound effect upon their approach to life.

Xerxes had been reared in a strongly competitive environment. Achievement, no matter what the cost, was the goal. Expressions of love were conditional upon his parents' approval of his actions. Xerxes, therefore, had grown to manhood having been deprived of the unconditional love and acceptance of his parents. Furthermore, the competition was keen. Xerxes was not Darius' eldest son, and only one could succeed their father and sit on his throne.

Esther, on the other hand, had been left an orphan when both her parents had died. She was also a "stranger" in a "strange land." Any feelings of abandonment, isolation, or worthlessness she may have felt were countered by the unconditional acceptance and positive love given her by Mordecai (2:7). She emerged from the trauma of loss with a sense of worth that gave her confidence as she faced unexpected events in her life.

A Study in Contrasts

In coming together as husband and wife, Xerxes and Esther were total opposites. They had nothing in common. Their lives illustrate, however, how a wife may be lovingly supportive of her husband and be treated by him as his "queen" (2:17). The secret lies in an understanding of the meaning of the little word *l-o-v-e*.

Xerxes needed a positive, unconditional, affirming, loving wife (something all men need!). He needed someone to fill the void that existed in his life.

When this love-need was not met—as happened during the interval between his deposition of Vashti and his return from Greece—an imbalance occurred. He suffered from a love hunger. There was no one with whom he could have a meaningful relationship. Evidence of his sense of deprivation may be seen in his fitful and irrational behavior whenever his plans did not succeed.

Esther, on the other hand, did not suffer from this deficiency. She was able to maintain healthy relationships with others, even when she did not receive positive affirmation for extended periods of time (Est. 2:12 where she was separated from Mordecai for a full year; and 4:11 where she had not been called into Xerxes' presence for a whole month).

On the Plus Side

As we continue to apply the principle of love within a relationship to the situation before us, we find that Esther loved from within her being. She was internally motivated. Xerxes, however, was moved to demonstrate his love when prompted by external circumstances (5:1–2, 6; 7:2ff.).

This contrast in the conduct of Xerxes and Esther leads us to conclude that:

- A truly loving nature is nonpossessive and admiring, rather than needing; it makes few requests, is never demanding, and is nearly always pleasure giving.
- True love can never be completely expended or completely satiated. It has inherent within it the dynamic of growth as well as a zest for life.
- The benefits of this kind of love are widespread and pervasive. They affect every area of life.
- The person whose love emanates from within receives satisfaction from giving; the person whose need for love stems from an internal deficiency finds gratification to be external to himself, in things like admiration, possessions, and sex for its own sake, for example.
- In real love, there is an absence of anxiety or hostility. (Any "anxiety" that is present is for the happiness or pleasure of the other person.)

- Those with a strong, internal desire for the other person's well-being are less dependent upon others and, therefore, more autonomous; less jealous and, therefore, more trusting. They are less needful and more inclined to be spontaneous. They are also more likely to be encouraging of their spouse, proud of his/her accomplishments, altruistic, and generous.
- In the persons who love from their inner beings, there is more likely to be a congruence between their mind and emotions, with the result that balanced motivation can be given to the will.[5]

Mature love builds up our marriage partner (1 Cor. 13:4–8). It increases our spouse's sense of worth and provides a secure basis upon which to develop a growing relationship. It also becomes the one sure foundation for the rearing of happy, healthy children.

Interaction

1. Imagine you are Hegai, the chief eunuch. Over three hundred attractive young girls from many different nations have just arrived in Susa. You are responsible for them. What would cause you to take special notice of one of these girls named Esther? How does she differ from the others?

2. Virginia Ramey Mollenkott, in her preface to Paul Jewett's *Man as Male and Female*, says: ". . . if woman must of necessity be subordinate [to man], she must of necessity be inferior" (p. 8). In contrast to Dr. Mollenkott's statement, the Bible stresses *mutual* submission (Eph. 5:21) without either person fearing that one is inferior to the other.

In the context of the story of Esther, it should be borne in mind that Vashti was deposed because she refused to submit to Xerxes' immodest and irresponsible request (Est. 1:10–22). Xerxes was wrong, of course, but her refusal was graceless and exposed her husband to public humiliation.

Esther, on the other hand, had a totally different attitude. Do you think that her relationship with Xerxes deprived her of her individuality (Est. 5; 7)? Why?

Note that such was Esther's influence upon Xerxes that *he* submitted to her (Est. 8:3–8). Why do you think he did this? Do the events of chapter 8 indicate the kind of influence a godly wife may have on her husband? What principles may modern wives and husbands draw from this story?

3. What are the unique kinds of problems facing a second wife? How may she best grapple with her husband's feelings toward, or memories of, his first wife? What can we learn from Esther's attitude toward Xerxes that may be of help to someone in a similar situation today?

4. It frequently happens in counseling that a wife complains of her husband's immaturity (or vice versa). The external evidences of this are many: unrealistic ideals, being overly dependent on the opinions of others, a lack of emotional stability, impulsivity, forgetting commitments, making excuses, etc. When these symptoms are present, what should a wife (or husband) do? Illustrate your answer with details from the Book of Esther.

5. In considering *true* love, take 1 Corinthians 13:4–8 and see how many of the specifics mentioned by the apostle Paul find a parallel in the attitude or conduct of Esther. What does her example teach us?

9

The Search for Common Values

*When love is at its best, one loves
So much that he cannot forget.*
—Helen Hunt Jackson

People generally marry because they believe they will be happier married rather than single. They feel they will be more contented sharing their lives with someone rather than living by themselves. They believe that having a person to whom they can impart their innermost dreams and desires is preferable to striving to reach goals and objectives without having anyone to rejoice with them over their accomplishments.

We have never met anyone who married with the intention of becoming unhappy or miserable. The question before us, however, is, Why, then, are there so many unhappy marriages? What led Judge J. M. Woolsey, in a historic case, to describe marriage as a "status of antagonistic cooperation . . . [in which] centripetal and centrifugal forces are continuously at work . . ."?[1]

With such contrary forces operating within a relationship, it is no wonder that many people have turned from advocating marriage to being skeptical of it. Writers have variously described the union of a man and woman as a "fetter" or a "snare,"[2] a "cure for love's intoxication,"[3] or likened it to a "lottery ticket which cannot be torn up if you lose."[4]

At best, most would agree with the unknown writer of *Politenphuia:* "Marriage with peace is this world's paradise; with strife, this life's purgatory."

The questions all of us wish to have answered, therefore, are: How may marriages be made happy? Given the fact that trials and tensions will continue because they are part of life, how may a couple enjoy rest and peace within their relationship?

FROM DELIGHT TO DISAPPOINTMENT

It may at first surprise us that the answer to these questions comes from a consideration of the marriage of Hosea and Gomer. Their experience of unhappiness differs little from the experiences of countless couples today. The book recounts the story of a broken vow and a broken home, the shattered hopes of God's prophet, and the wasted life of his wife.

The story is set in the city of Samaria. Hosea is a young preacher. At the height of his promising career, he is instructed by God to go and do a most unusual thing: he is to marry a prostitute.

Because the story does not fit our neat, tidy categories of what is "acceptable" in Sunday school curricula or "proper subject material" for pulpit exposition, we have shunned the Book of Hosea. God, however, chose to include this story in His Word to reveal an important truth: *Our marriage should be an earthly reflection of our relationship with Him.*

If we are having difficulty communicating with our spouse, it may be that the lines of communication with the Lord are broken down. If our relationship lacks satisfaction, it may be His intent to show us that He derives no satisfaction from His relationship with us. If we spend most of our time enduring a "cold war," it may be His way of showing us that we have incurred His enmity.

The point is that the horizontal relationship of marriage is designed by God to reflect our vertical relationship with Him. Or, put differently, the quality of our union with Him may be reflected in the state of our union with our spouse. The more our marriage (or even the attitude of one partner) reflects the outlook of society, the more likely is this to be true.

Tough Realities

Does such a view of marriage surprise us? Consider the way in which Hosea's marriage paralleled the spiritual condition of the people of his day (Hos. 1:2, 4–9). Even the births of his children were given special significance and portrayed the spiritual condition of Israel before the Lord. As confirmation of this, notice God's words in chapter 3:

> "Go, again, love a woman who is loved by her husband, yet an adulteress, *even as the Lord loves the sons of Israel*, though they turn to other gods . . . ." (Hos. 3:1, emphasis added)

There is a similar kind of parallelism expressed by the Apostle Paul. He wrote:

> For the husband is the head of the wife, as Christ is the head of the church . . . ; as the church is subject to Christ, so also wives [ought to be subject] to their husbands. . . . Husbands, love your wives, just as Christ also loved the church. . . . For this cause a man shall leave his father and mother, and shall cleave to his wife; and the two shall be one flesh. *This is a great mystery; but I am speaking in reference to Christ and the church.* (Eph. 5:23–25, 31–32, emphasis added)

We also find Peter linking the quality of the relationship between a husband and wife with the quality of their spiritual life. He ties this directly to the answers to prayer that they receive (1 Peter 3:7).

While this may at first seem to be a strange and new teaching, its seeming novelty and lack of conformity to what we have usually thought about marriage is probably due to our neglect of this portion of God's Word.

We believe that a clear understanding of the teaching of the Book of Hosea underscores the vital link between the quality of the relationship between a husband and wife and the state of one's spiritual relationship with the Lord.

Grass Roots Corruption

The woman whom Hosea marries has willingly given her body to gratify the passions of vile and impure men. She is a most unpromising candidate for a preacher's home.

Because hope springs eternal in the human heart, Hosea probably hopes that his love for Gomer will woo her from her wantonness. But the home he provides for her and the unconditional acceptance he gives her do not curb her corruption. As soon as he leaves the home to go about his work, she too leaves to join her paramours. She is clever in her deception of him, and he does not find out about her affairs for several years.

The point of the contrast in lifestyles is that as Hosea spends his days trying to turn the nation from the path of destruction, his wife (who typifies the nation) spends her days in betrayal of his love and in violation of her vows. In a very real sense, she is bent on self-destruction.

It might be advanced by some that perhaps Hosea did not spend sufficient time with his pleasure-loving wife; that he spent too much time trying to convert the nation and not enough time trying to win his wife to the Lord.

This may be so, even though the text of Scripture does not even hint at its possibility. What does appear obvious is that Gomer did not share the same concerns or values as her husband. She did not uphold him in his work. Whatever he did, he did without her participation, support, or encouragement. She failed, therefore, in her role as his helpmeet.

Uncovering the Facts

In the course of time, Gomer shares with Hosea her pending maternity. She is expecting a baby, and Hosea assumes he is the father.

He is aware of Gomer's estrangement from him in all that he holds dear and probably hopes that God will use this infant to bring them closer to one another. And when Gomer's son is born and lies helplessly in her arms, Hosea may have wished that in some way this child would reach out his chubby arms and draw their lives together.

If Gomer showed any change of character following the birth of her son, it was short-lived. In the course of time, she conceives again. This time she gives birth to a daughter. A year or two later she bears another son. Then a dark shadow falls over Hosea. Gomer leaves him, deserting her children. She returns to her lovers.

Was there a flare-up in the home? Did she leave him a note on the kitchen table or in their bedroom? We do not know. Did Hosea go after her? Was it then that he learned to his horror that his children—those born in his house—bore a resemblance to Gomer's admirers? Did he suddenly realize that her children are not his after all (Hos. 2:4–5)?

He did learn the truth, and the blow must have been heavy and severe. It must have caused him intense emotional pain. He returned home and asked his children to plead with their mother to return to them. But their efforts were of no avail.

Single Parent, Double Trouble

The days pass slowly. They lengthen into weeks, then years. Hosea contents himself with rearing Gomer's children, while all the time continuing to minister to the nation.

Did his neighbors laugh at him behind his back? Did they use Gomer's defection as an excuse to reject his words? Did some of those women, long single, think that now Hosea might divorce Gomer and marry one of them?

Gomer may have left Hosea's home, but she has not left his heart. Her departure has made his work difficult. He, however, perseveres in doing what is right. His love for her never wavers.

Confusion Over Values

It is probable that Gomer was lured away from Hosea with the promise of gifts and the thought of bettering herself (Hos. 2:5). In chapter 2, God links very closely His relationship with the nation and Hosea's conduct toward Gomer. What is certain is that she imagined she would be better off as a "high society hooker" than as the wife of a lowly prophet. Little did she realize that, as with the "prodigal son" of Luke 15, the path she was treading led downhill. In her case, it literally led straight to the gutter.

In the course of time, Gomer finds that she can no longer attract the rich and prosperous to her boudoir (2:5–7). She, therefore, seeks the services of one who will obtain clients for her. Eventually, he owns her, and when her beauty has faded and she is no longer desirable, he sells her (3:1–2).

Hosea follows Gomer's downward slide. When he learns of her destitution, he seeks out her "pimp" and gives him money and provisions to take to her (2:8). He hopes that his lovingkindness will cause her to return to him. Gomer, however, is not told that it is Hosea who has given her the gifts.

Instead, she imagines that the false gods, Baal and Asherah, have prospered her; and she worships them (v. 13).

Rethinking and Unthinkable

Now, before we pronounce our anathemas upon Gomer, let us remember that, as with the prodigal son in Christ's parable, we have been playing the part of Gomer in our relationship with the Lord. We have spent our lives following after the things of this world. We have taken His gifts for granted. We have spurned His grace. We have turned our backs on His love and indulged ourselves in the allurement of riches. We have lightly esteemed His blessings and have felt that, by going our own way, we could find greater satisfaction in life.

If we are honest with ourselves, we will have to admit that materialism, vanity, and the pursuit of pleasure have seduced us away from our devotion to the Lord. Yet He continues to surround us with countless benefits of His love. As with Hosea of old, He wants to hear us say, "I will go back to my first husband, for it was better for me then than now" (Hos. 2:7; see also Luke 15:17–20, and in relation to Christ and believers, Eph. 5:32).

Persistence Pays Off

All of Hosea's efforts to win back Gomer fail (Hos. 2). He, therefore, withdraws. Sin will have to run its relentless course. Gomer will have to experience the "desert" phase of her folly (vv. 3, 10–13).

In the story, Gomer experiences hard times. The man who now owns her is unable to secure sufficient customers for her. He becomes desperate when he can no longer make enough money off her to buy food. No one, it seems, wants her any more. He, therefore, decides to sell her into slavery.

God informs Hosea that Gomer is to be sold and instructs him to attend the auction. Hosea stands in the crowd watching the degrading spectacle. One by one, those to be sold are dragged to the front. Some of the young men are doubtless bought for their strength. Some of the pretty young girls are purchased by wealthy men to wait on their wives.

Finally, Gomer's turn arrives. She is dirty. Her hair is disheveled, and she has the look of hopelessness written on her face. The bidding starts. "Ten pieces of silver? Who will give me ten pieces of silver for this woman?" There is a pause.

The starting bid is accepted. Someone else bids eleven. Hosea offers twelve. Most slaves would sell for at least thirty shekels of silver (Lev. 27:4). Hosea hopes that the bidding will not go much higher for the prophet could not compete with the wealthy at the auction.

The auctioneer coaxes those gathered about him. "Am I bid thirteen? Thirteen shekels of silver for this (his words trail off as he looks at Gomer) . . . woman."

Someone bids thirteen shekels. "Fourteen," says another standing within the group. There is a slight pause. The auctioneer's gavel begins to rise. "Fifteen," says Hosea. All heads turn in his direction. He feels very conspicuous.

Then someone says half jokingly, "Fifteen, and a homer of barley."

Hosea is desperate. His hands are sweaty. His mouth is dry.

"Going . . . going . . ." says the auctioneer.

"Wait!" says Hosea. "Fifteen shekels of silver and a homer and a half of barley."

There is some laughter at so strange a bid.

"Gone!" says the auctioneer, "to the preacher over there." Then turning, he says, "Next we have . . .", and the auction continues with no thought of the people whose lives are being bought and sold with such disaffection.

"This Slave's My Wife"

Hosea, however, has purchased Gomer. She is now his legal possession.

As he leads her away, he does not give her the tongue-lashing she deserves. Instead, he assures her of his love (Hos. 3:3). She still is his wife. He has redeemed her from a life of slavery. Now that she knows where her sin has led her, she will no longer wish to go running after other lovers. She will remain in his home many days. This will give the idle gossip of the people time to die down. Then they will be seen together in public again.

BLUEPRINT FOR A HAPPY UNION

As we begin to apply the teaching of these chapters to our own situation, we find that it illustrates the importance of a healthy union—the kind of union that should exist between a husband and his wife.

Permanent Benefits

"But what benefits," we may ask, "are we to glean from this story? It happened long ago. It also concerns Israel, not the church. What possible relevance can it have to us?"

Dr. G. Campbell Morgan anticipated our questions. As he pointed out, "God interprets Himself to us through our own experiences."[5] The kinship that exists between a husband and wife parallels in the Old Testament the vital connection between God and Israel; and in the New Testament, the union of Christ and His Church (Isa. 54:6; Jer. 31:1-10, 14; Eph. 5:21-33). The kinds of problems that impair our relationship with the Godhead frequently are mirrored in the difficulties that arise in our marriages. Paul spoke of this truth as a mystery (Eph. 5:32).

In the case of Hosea and Gomer, we find first that Gomer had a very deficient view of the true God. Initially, if she believed in Him at all, it probably was as a distant deity who was unconcerned about her. This made it easy for her to flaunt His moral laws. Her lack of true spiritual sensitivity also made it easy for her to engage in idolatry (Hos. 2:11–13). At least Baal could be seen and promised her success.

Gomer's lack of interest in spiritual realities had its outworking in her failure to be supportive of her husband in his work. In addition, her insensitivity to eternal realities made it easy for her to gratify her emotionally immature desires. She sinned against Hosea by committing adultery. Her self-centeredness can also be seen in her willful desertion of her children (Hos. 2:5).

Sexual Confusion

Second, when we, like Gomer, lack a strong, internal God-consciousness, we have a deficient sense of our worth. This deficiency is carried over into our relationship with others.

In the case of Gomer, she sold her body for the sake of feeling wanted by someone. The money she received, she spent on herself in order to try and make herself feel attractive. As her beauty began to fade, she ardently pursued those who formerly had been happy to associate with her (Hos. 2:5, 7). They, however, no longer found her desirable.

Sad, disillusioned, and lonely, Gomer sank lower and lower in her feelings about herself. She felt alienated from God and alienated also from her husband, for he was a prophet of God. She had sought a life of pleasure and now felt herself spurned by her former lovers, disgraced in the sight of others, destitute, and without hope in the world (v. 10).

God, however, in grace wooed Gomer to Himself. In time, He would also reconcile her to her husband.

Wooing the Wayward

In our relationship with God, we often find that He allows our willfulness to bring us to the end of ourselves—our wisdom, our ability, our resourcefulness. With no one to turn to, we are compelled to turn to Him.

This was Gomer's experience. In her extremity, when she was being sold as a slave, the Lord opened for her a "door of hope" (Hos. 2:15). This reference to a "door of hope" takes us back to Joshua, chapter 7. There, the "valley of Achor," or valley of trouble, was associated with affliction. The sin of Achan had brought trouble on Israel. As a result of what happened to Achan, all Israel had a new concept of the righteousness and justice of God; and from that time onward, the name of the valley served to remind them of their accountability to Him.

In His sovereign grace, *God promises to make the place of our extremity a door of hope*. In Gomer's experience, He intervened. He sent Hosea to buy her (3:1). Apparently, God knew that she was now ready to turn from the evils of the past to faith in Him and fidelity to her husband.

Hosea obediently bought Gomer, but what would he now be like as her husband? She had spurned every token of his love (2:5, 8–9). Could she now complain, if he treated her harshly?

Coming Back

Of vital importance in any form of restoration is *forgiveness*. This is true whenever we seek to set things right with the Lord and to receive again the blessings that accompany our obedience to His revealed will.

Forgiveness is important, too, in our relationship with our spouse. As we seek to understand the mind of the Lord on this matter, let us consider Hosea's attitude toward Gomer. He might have reasoned that it was a mistake to have married her in the first place. All she had ever brought him was trouble. She had even deceived him into thinking that he was the father of her children. Due to her willful waywardness, his task as a preacher of righteousness had been changed from very difficult to virtually impossible. Now God wanted him to go and buy her at the slave market. "In no way!" he might have reasoned. "She's finally gotten what she deserved."

This could have been Hosea's response, but it was not. He exemplified the spirit of forgiveness.

Reconciliation, however, involved discipline for Gomer (Hos. 3:3–5)—not harsh, authoritarian discipline, but practical discipline. She had to refrain from all sexual relationships, even with Hosea, so that when they did engage in intimate expressions of love, it might be with the past behind them, with renewed desires for one another kindled in their hearts, and with a new realization of their oneness.

In forgiving Gomer, Hosea illustrates for us the kind of attitude that should characterize us in our dealings with each other (Matt. 6:14–15; Eph. 4:32). Hosea brought her back to their home with due respect for her person. He did not threaten her or heap abuse upon her. He accepted her.

Hosea also graciously established the parameters of their relationship. He did not "lay down the law"; neither did he preach to her. He exemplified the grace of God in his attitude and conduct.

As we reflect on Hosea 2:14–20, we find that God had already spoken similar words of acceptance and assurance to Israel (note vv. 16, 19–20). Their relationship would not compromise the truth. Instead, it would be *based upon righteousness and justice, lovingkindness and compassion, faithfulness and understanding.*

This is the way God also relates to us; and it is the way we, too, should relate to one another. Forgiveness and reconciliation pave the way for restoration in a relationship. But there is more.

Important Promise

To those who willingly walk in His ways, the Lord promises that there will again be answers to prayer (Hos. 2:21–22). Furthermore, as a result of these answered prayers, God's people will be able to respond in praise and worship (v. 23).

It is significant that the Lord Jesus said that wherever two or three meet together in His name (and where is this more natural than in a home?), there He will be in their midst. He also promised that if two people agree in prayer regarding anything, it will be done for them by His Father (Matt. 18:19–20). And where is prayer more likely to take place than in a home, where a godly couple unite to pray about their mutual concerns? Peter, however, warned that dissension in the home will cause our prayers to go unanswered (1 Peter 3:7). We, therefore, need to develop true *unity,* so that our prayers might continue to be answered.

True unity is centered in Christ, not ourselves. Centrifugal and centripetal forces are continuously at work in our homes. Gomer illustrates how easily a person's life may begin to gravitate away from the center—from the unifying principles of marriage—and with predictable results.

On the other hand, God shows through His counsel of Israel the kind of centripetal forces that contribute toward true unity. And Hosea illustrates for us the attitudes of righteousness and justice, lovingkindness and compassion, faithfulness and understanding, attitudes that should accompany forgiveness and restoration.

There are two things we need to remember: (1) No matter how bad our present situation, God can open a "door of hope" for us; and (2) the real blessings of marriage are experienced when *both* the husband and wife are rightly related to the Lord and to one another.

Interaction

1. Hosea ministered in a time of great prosperity for the northern tribes of Israel (Hos. 1:1; *c.* 755–710 B.C.). In this respect, the society of his day differed little from ours today. The rich hoarded their riches and oppressed the poor. From your consideration of what is specifically mentioned (or else alluded to) in chapters 1 to 3, reconstruct the attitude and/or conduct of the people of his day. How would you describe their God-consciousness?

2. Building upon your observations to question 1, discuss the centrifugal effect such attitudes had upon the spiritual climate of the day. In what ways were these attitudes mirrored in Hosea's marriage?

Centrifugal forces in society that detract from the development of a true God-consciousness also have a detrimental effect upon the home. Brainstorm on some of the ways in which centripetal forces—where the movement is directed toward the center—might be used to counteract these destructive centrifugal influences present in our society.

3. A healthy marriage should be characterized as a "holy triangle." It should be God-centered and other-directed. Share with one another some of the difficulties we all face as

we try to make this a reality in our lives. What are the benefits (a) to us, and (b) to our children?

4. As you reflect on Gomer's experience at the slave market and her purchase by Hosea, consider the New Testament teaching of redemption. Redemption pictures us as individuals sold under sin's dominion with no power in and of ourselves to remedy or alter our state. Christ, however, has paid the price of our redemption with His own blood, which He freely offered up for us all. His offer, however, must be accepted by us individually. He then sets us free so that we may serve Him out of hearts filled with gratitude.

How can a husband and wife, as redeemed people, join together to show their love for the Lord and their willing service to Him?

5. Because we are all imperfect beings, we constantly need one another's forgiveness. Consider the issues involved in Gomer's reconciliation to Hosea (based upon God's desire for Israel; see Hos. 2:19–20). Does the fact that her children are not mentioned in 3:1–5 give us reason to believe that they were already grown? If so, then what did Gomer forfeit as a result of her sinful ways?

10

Is Real Unity in Marriage Possible?

Wicked mirth never true pleasure brings,
But honest minds are pleased with honest things.
—Francis Beaumont

We tend to think of Joseph and Mary only at Christmas time. For thirty minutes on the Sunday before Christmas, we listen as our pastor preaches on the birth of Christ from one of the well-known passages in the Gospels.

Our attention, of course, is rightly focused upon the Lord Jesus. Perhaps some mention is made of Mary, but virtually none of Joseph. He is regarded as a necessary appendage to the story—something similar to fathers today whose usefulness is limited to earning the family income and paying the bills. And so it is that Joseph is impolitely passed by.

In reality, the marriage of Joseph and Mary is one of the most significant in all of the Scriptures. They were the couple selected by God the Father to rear His Son. Their relationship created the atmosphere of the home in which the Lord Jesus continued to grow and become strong, to increase in wisdom, and to enjoy the grace of God upon His life (Luke 2:40, 52).

This atmosphere in the home was possible because the marriage of Joseph and Mary was characterized by unity. Their unity stemmed from a commitment to each other and to the will of God. Their unity also grew through a series of circumstances that seemed to heap upon them one form after another of trial or difficulty.

THE CRITERIA OF A GOOD WIFE

The story begins, chronologically, with Mary (Luke 1:26–38). She is about fourteen years of age and betrothed to a youthful carpenter, about three or four years her senior. His name is Joseph.

Ancient Customs

Betrothal in oriental countries was a more solemn form of commitment than engagements today (Deut. 22:23–27). Dr. William Barclay explains the three stages of a Jewish marriage:

> First, *there was the engagement*. The engagement was often made when the couple were only children. It was usually made through the parents, or through a professional match-maker. And it was often made without the couple involved ever having seen each other. Marriage was held to be far too serious a step to be left to the dictates of human passion and the human heart.
>
> Second, *there was the betrothal*. The betrothal was what we might call the ratification of the engagement into which the couple had previously entered. At this point, the engagement, entered into by the parents or the match-maker, could be broken if the girl was unwilling to go on with it. But once the betrothal was entered into, it was absolutely binding. It lasted for one year. During that year the couple were known as man and wife, although they had not the rights of man and wife. It could not be terminated in any other way than by divorce. In the Jewish law we frequently find what is to us a curious phrase. A girl whose fiancé had died during the year

of betrothal is called "a virgin who is a widow." It was at this stage that Joseph and Mary were. They were betrothed, and if Joseph wished to end the betrothal, he could do so in no other way than by divorce; and in that year of betrothal Mary was legally known as his wife.

The third stage was the marriage proper, which took place at the end of the year of betrothal.[1]

Angelic Visitation

It is during the second phase of Joseph and Mary's marital relationship that the angel Gabriel is sent from God to Mary. He informs her that she has been selected to be the mother of Israel's long-awaited Messiah (Luke 1:30–36). The whole scene, as well as the actual words that transpire between them, is of the utmost importance to us.

Several things are told us about Mary that, when combined, make her an ideal wife and mother.

She is chaste (v. 27). Mary is twice referred to as a virgin. The evils of her society and the close proximity of a Roman garrison (with its ready money to those willing to sacrifice virtue for a few shekels), have had no effect upon her. She has retained her purity. Hers is a positive form of righteousness.

She is in touch with her emotions (vv. 28–29). Mary experiences fear, yet is not being overcome by it. Even while Gabriel is speaking to her, she is able to keep in perspective the events that are taking place. And the fact that she reflects upon his words before reaching a decision indicates that she is self-determining (2:19).

She is a woman of integrity. Mary's manner of life has caused her to find favor with God. She is, therefore, in a position to receive His blessings as well as to do good to all who come into contact with her (v. 30).[2]

She is a woman of faith. After hearing Gabriel's announcements (vv. 31–33), Mary does not doubt the veracity of his words, but only questions the means whereby they will be fulfilled (v. 34).

Mary submits to the will of God with a remarkable display of poise and an absence of concern for herself (v. 38).

For many of us, an announcement such as the one Mary received would have caused us instant panic! When will this happen? How will I explain my condition to my parents, neighbors, and friends? What will they think of me? How will I explain all this to Joseph? Will he still marry me? What will happen to me if no one believes me?

Rather than wrestle with these overwhelming questions, Mary chooses rather to rest in the Lord and allow Him to work out the details in her life. Her trust in Him is as complete as her submission.

Appeal for Understanding

Sometime soon after she has conceived, Mary decides to go and visit Elizabeth (Luke 1:36). She feels the need for her relative's mature counsel and understanding. Traveling, perhaps in the company of friends of her parents who are journeying south to Jerusalem, she makes her way to the hill country of Judah (vv. 39ff.).

Mary spends a happy three months in Elizabeth's company. Then, just before Elizabeth's baby is born, Mary returns to Nazareth. The evidence of her pregnancy is beginning to show, and, as Matthew describes the situation, "on her return, she is found to be with child" (Matt. 1:18).

Imagine Joseph's reaction when he greets his fiancée and finds that she is carrying someone else's baby. Jim Bishop, in his book *The Day Christ Was Born,* describes the scene for us:

The shock to Joseph was beyond measure. Throughout the courtship his intended bride had worn an aura of innocence; he was painfully conscious of her lack of knowledge. She had gone away three months ago, and now she [has] returned . . . pregnant.

It is impossible to read the depths of sorrow in both hearts. He looked at her tenderly and she offered no word of explanation. She looked away from him and wished that she might tell everything. The baby was going to need a foster-father—who better than the man she loved, the gentle and pious Joseph?[3]

The choice, however, would have to be his. But how could she tell him what had happened to her? Her conception by the Holy Spirit seemed too incredible to be true.

THE CHARACTER OF A GOOD HUSBAND

Joseph returns home in a state of bewilderment. He feels that Mary, the one whom he loves more than anyone else in the world, has betrayed him. His heart is so heavy that he can scarcely bear the pain. He needs time to think, to pray. He needs the kind of help and comfort that only God can give. In agony of mind, he wrestles with the facts.

A Hard Choice

Some other person in a similar situation might have thrust Mary away in indignation. He might also have been tempted to hurt her and put her to open shame as he felt he had been hurt and put to shame. It is difficult to think clearly when one is hurting emotionally. The pain is so great that it clogs the wheels of reason.

Finally, Joseph reaches a decision. Dr. Alexander Whyte describes it for us:

> ... there was only one course left open to him. Take her to his home he could not, but neither could he consent to make Mary a public example, and there was only left to him the sad enough step of putting her away privily.[4]

The Scripture attributes Joseph's choice to his righteous nature. He is a just man. Instead of having Mary judicially condemned and punished, or given a bill of divorce before witnesses, he chooses to "put her away privately" (Matt. 1:19). It is a most gracious and humane course of action.

Husband of the Year

It is only after Joseph has reached his decision to shield Mary from shameful exposure, that the events of Matthew 1:20ff. occur. In his sleep—perhaps his first restful night since learning of Mary's condition—an angel of the Lord appears to him. He is greeted as David's "son," his descendant, and told to proceed with his marriage plans. He is given assurance that Mary has not betrayed him. Her conception is of the Holy Spirit. Though Mary's child will not be his, marriage to Mary will give the child legal status. Her child will then have title to David's throne (Matt. 1:20).

Further indication of the uniqueness of Mary's Son and of the nature of His work is indicated by the name Joseph is to give Him: Jesus. The explanation ("for it is He who will save His people from their sins" [Matt. 1:21]) fills Joseph's heart with joy.

On hearing the angel's words, Joseph obeys. He arises and makes the necessary plans for his marriage to Mary to be formalized by bringing her officially to his home. He also restrains himself from having sexual relations with her until after Jesus has been born[5] (Matt. 1:22–25).

Deeper Issues

Charles H. Spurgeon, in his comments on this passage, points to the necessity for the virgin conception and birth of Christ.

> [This] is a deep, mysterious, and delicate subject, fitter for reverent faith than for speculative curiosity. The Holy Ghost wrought, in the chosen virgin, the body of our Lord. There was no other way of his being born; for had he been of a sinful father, how should he have possessed a sinless nature? He is born of a woman, that he might be human; but not by man, that he might not be sinful.[6]

God the Father, in His infinite wisdom, took care that the Lord Jesus, for the purpose of accomplishing our salvation, had a human body (Heb. 2:9, 14–15). He was also entirely free from sin (Heb. 7:26). In this way, through His death, He could atone for the sins of His people (Heb. 9:11–15).

In addition, by being adopted formally by Joseph (Luke 2:21), the Lord Jesus became legal heir to the throne of David.

What Manner of Man?

These considerations lead us to ask what kind of man God the Father chose to be the foster-father of His Son.

From the record in Matthew 1:18–25, we glean the following facts about Joseph.

He was a just man—the kind of person who, in spite of his poverty and the penchant of those about him to take advantage of a given situation, was absolutely honest in his business dealings. He gave full value for the money received.

Mary knew that Joseph was trustworthy. God the Father knew that he could be entrusted with the rearing of Jesus.

He was a considerate man—the kind of person whose concern for others (even when he felt they may have wronged him) took precedence over all thought for himself. This characteristic, as we shall see, was not confined to a solitary instance, but continued throughout his life (Luke 2). He modelled practical goodness for his children.

He was an obedient man. He had the courage to act at once upon the information the Lord gave him (Matt. 1:20–24; 2:13–15, 19–23). His obedience was always judicious and complete. He fully carried out each divine directive. However, when the information given him left room for independent action, his decisions were in accordance with what was best for his family (Matt. 2:19, 22–23).

Such characteristics make a wife feel secure. They also provide a stable environment in which a couple may rear their children.

THE VULNERABILITY FACTOR

As we continue to follow the experiences of Joseph and Mary, we gain new insights into their characters as well as the circumstances they face (Matt. 2:1–23; Luke 2:1–40).

Malicious Gossip

The first trial Mary and Joseph face as a couple is the stigma of Mary's having conceived Jesus out of wedlock (John 8:41). It appears as if the Jews will not forget that Mary was pregnant at the time Joseph took her into his home.

The gossip was probably inevitable. The slander of their characters, however, is harder to bear. They are both righteous before God, yet how can they explain to others what really happened? Who will believe them?

A couple for whom the approval of others is all-important would have found themselves growing apart under such relentless opposition. The husband would begin to doubt his wife's story and, in time, as pressure mounted, begin to blame her for their misfortunes. Such a spirit of divisiveness, when combined with evidence of their individual insecurity, would eventually drive a wedge between them.

Joseph and Mary, however, know the truth. Their union is strengthened as they persevere with their God-appointed task. Let others criticize and malign them; in their hearts they know they are right. The adversity they experience draws them closer together.

New Trials

Shortly before the Lord Jesus is born, Joseph and Mary find themselves compelled to go to Bethlehem for a census. Caesar Augustus has learned that his subjects are not paying their taxes. He, therefore, instructs his officials to enroll all his subjects so that proper taxation may be effected. For Joseph and Mary to go to Bethlehem, the city of David, to take part in the census is not convenient. Mary is far advanced in her pregnancy. The Romans, however, who rule the civilized world of that time, are not interested in the convenience of their subjects. As a result, Joseph and Mary are compelled to leave Galilee and journey to Judah.

Jim Bishop describes the scene on the road south:

> [Mary] felt no pain. This was the fifth day from Nazareth and, from hour to hour, she had progressed from tiredness to fatigue to weariness to the deep anesthesia of exhaustion. . . . She no longer noticed the chafe of the goatskin against her leg, nor the sway of the food bag on the other side of the

animal. Her veiled head hung and she saw millions of pebbles on the road.[7]

That night Joseph probably makes a comfortable bed for Mary in the open. They are saving what little money they have for the baby. It is cold, and Joseph and Mary huddle together for warmth. The next day they move on again. The road is busy. Innumerable people are making their way to and from Jerusalem. Each is occupied with his own concerns; each is anxious to register and return to the difficult task of earning a living.

After passing through Jerusalem, Joseph and Mary make their way slowly to Bethlehem. It is only six miles south of the capital, but the road seems interminably long. It has been a hot day. They are tired and thirsty. Mary is uncomfortable. The baby has dropped in His position. Birth can only be a few hours away.

As they approach the village of Bethlehem, they are surprised to see so many people. The dusty road is lined by those who have been unable to find accommodation in the city. Joseph consoles Mary. He will find a place for them. And with this, he coaxes the ass to walk a little faster.

The rest of the story of that night is well-known. Every available place of rest is occupied. In response to Joseph's earnest entreaty, the innkeeper permits them to use a cave that he has converted into a stable. And there, with the acrid odor of the stall filling the night air, by the light of a single wick lamp, with only the glistening-eyed stare of the animals for company, Christ is born.

Does Joseph act as a midwife? We do not know. No one, it seems, cares about the young couple. No one brings them any food. They are all too preoccupied with the census.

The Uses of Adversity

The hardships Joseph and Mary face draw them closer together. In a very real sense, their lives are Christ-centered. They are committed to doing all that God the Father wants done. This has a unifying effect upon them, and their relationship is strengthened because of it.

Visits and Visitations

Luke tells the beautiful story of those who are the first to spread the news of Christ's birth (Luke 2:8–20). Shepherds come and visit Him. Then, some weeks later, when Joseph has secured a small home for the family to live in, Matthew records the visit of the wise men (Matt. 2:1–12).

Following the departure of the magi, Joseph has a dream. An angel warns him of Herod's evil plan and instructs him to take the Child and His mother and to flee into Egypt (Matt. 2:13ff.).

Had Joseph been like some people today, he might have questioned the guidance being given him. After all, he might have reasoned, he had just begun to establish a modest reputation for himself in Bethlehem as a carpenter. What will people say when they return to pick up their repaired merchandise and find that he has left the country? Furthermore, it is not convenient to take a baby on such a long journey. And if God is really as powerful as he has been led to believe, why can He not find some other way to keep them safe from Herod?

Joseph was not like us. The Bible tells us, "And he arose and took the Child and His mother by night [with haste], and departed for Egypt" (Matt. 2:14). He is prompt and uncomplaining in his obedience.

Mary, too, goes along willingly. She does not question

the vision Joseph has received. In this, she shows her oneness with him. Their marriage is based upon mutual trust. Their relationship will grow stronger as a result of the experiences they are compelled to share.

"But We've Just Gotten Settled"

In Egypt, Joseph and Mary probably find acceptance with one of the large Jewish communities. No one there knows of the circumstances surrounding the birth of their Son or the reasons for their nocturnal flight. To the residents along the Nile, they are just another Jewish family. They are welcomed and, after the usual introductions and questions, settle down to become a part of the community.

It must have been with a sense of relief that Joseph and Mary escape the gossip of their neighbors in Nazareth and the capricious plots of Herod. Now, for the first time, they can settle down peaceably, establish themselves, and plan for the future.

Within two or three years, however, Joseph has another dream (Matt. 1:19ff). An angel of the Lord appears to him and tells him it is time for him to return to the land of Israel.

Was this welcome news? Did they find it easy to uproot themselves, leave their friends and return to the political tensions of Palestine? The biblical record merely says, "And [Joseph] arose and took the Child and His mother, and came into the land of Israel" (Matt. 1:20). Once again his obedience to the divine directive is prompt and complete.

Joseph, however, is a wise and practical man. When he hears that Archelaus is reigning in Judah, he knows that it will not be safe to reside there. He, therefore, chooses to return to Galilee, to their hometown of Nazareth, and there take up the work he had laid down at the time of the census.

OTHER FACTORS

But how did Mary handle all these changes? Mary, we know, is a woman of independent thought and judgment (Luke 1:34, 38; 2:19), who can take appropriate action when needed (1:39), and who, in time, will emerge as the spokesperson of the family (2:41–52, note v. 38). How then does she, as a young bride and mother, respond to each situation? In what ways does she contribute toward the development and maintenance of unity in her relationship with Joseph?

Exonerated

If Mary had experienced any feeling of guilt over her premarital pregnancy, each move would have aggravated the situation and she would have tended to blame herself (or her child) each time they faced some new form of adversity. She would also have tended to become defensive if criticized. The fact that she did neither tacitly shows her integrity. Her conscience was clear. She was, therefore, free to be lovingly supportive of her husband. This is hinted at in the text each time they were moved from one place to another. She willingly accompanied Joseph and never questioned his leadership.

Fitting Example

There can be no doubt that Mary's commitment to Joseph paved the way for the development of a spirit of oneness in their home. It would have been easy for her to become child-centered. After all, her Son was the Lord of glory.

From passages like Matthew 13:55–56, however, we

know that Mary and Joseph enjoyed normal conjugal relations. Other sons and daughters were born to them.[8] Each new arrival would require her special attention for a time, and each growing child would need to be assigned duties around the house or in the workshop.

Perfect harmony was not possible (John 7:5ff.). Unity, however, was attained in the home, and Joseph and Mary saw all their sons and daughters (all except for Jesus) happily married.

PERSONAL APPLICATION

From a consideration of the lives of Mary and Joseph, we learn the importance of a woman being *chaste, mature, honest, believing,* and *responsive,* if she is to be a good wife. A man should be *trustworthy, considerate, obedient to the Lord,* and *judicious,* if he is to be a good husband.

Possessed of these qualities, a husband and his wife will be able to establish a stable home life. The adversity they face will bring them closer together. Each can then be committed to the other and to maintaining their home.

As a result, their home can become a haven, their children will be able to grow to adulthood in a healthy environment, and they can enjoy the blessings of each other's confidence and companionship. What more could any couple desire?

Interaction

1. In his commentary *The Gospel According to Luke,* Dr. G. Campbell Morgan writes:

[Nazareth] was one of the largest cities of Galilee; and being where it was geographically, it was a place where Roman soldiers often tarried overnight, and Greek merchantmen put up in the caravansaries. Nazareth was a hotbed of corruption. . . . When Nathaniel said, "Can any good thing come out of Nazareth?" he spoke as one familiar with the place. (p. 19)

Mary and Joseph were both from Nazareth. They were both people of faith and honor as well as being God-fearing and wise. How does one acquire these characteristics? What contributed to the growth of Mary and Joseph's character?

2. Timber was scarce in Israel. A few stately cedars grew in the alkaline soil, but apart from isolated date palms and fig trees and occasional fruit orchards, the country did not produce good lumber. A carpenter, therefore, ranked at the bottom of the honorable professions.

Joseph was a carpenter and an honest man, never taking advantage of a situation or overcharging a customer or using inferior materials and then pretending that he had used the best. Jesus followed Joseph and also became a carpenter (Matt. 13:55; Mark 6:3). He took up the lowliest profession known to mankind. And Mary, with a growing number of mouths to feed, administered the family's finances.

Discuss together the tensions economic privation brings upon a growing family. What are some of the most common problems? How may these be resolved? May we derive comfort from a knowledge that the Lord Jesus knew hardship at each stage of His life? Why? What rewards— temporal and spiritual—do you think Joseph and Mary received? How did their situation shape their system of values?

3. Apply the characteristics Joseph and Mary exemplify to the question of family unity. What strengths do these

characteristics contribute to a marriage? Without each strength being balanced by complimentary characteristics, what problems may arise?

How do you think Joseph and Mary worked together to achieve harmony in their relationship?

4. Trace each instance of Joseph's receiving some divinely given message. Each consisted of a *revelation* and a *response*. How might he have treated each vision or angelic visitation? What can we learn from his experience?

5. Joseph used his personal discretion when the occasion warranted (Matt. 2:22–23). Bethlehem was too close to Archelaus (who lived in Jerusalem). What prompted Joseph to go north to Galilee, and once there, select Nazareth as the place in which to live?

11

The Value of a Good Wife

Demagogues are the mob's lacquays. —Diogenes

Before his death, Jacques Lipchitz (1892–1973) dedicated his monument of the family as the "Wellspring of Society, the Hope of the Future" to the people of Philadelphia. His sculptured work stands in an open business plaza. Like many modern artistic productions, this one at first appears confusing to the casual observer. It is a powerful, yet appalling image of entangled confusion—hands and breasts, heads and bodies are all intermingled. This mass of dismembered humanity is set on top of a pedestal and holds aloft another ponderous mass of disoriented forms representing modern society.

If Lipchitz was trying to emphasize the turmoil and confusion of family life today, he succeeded. Torn by external and internal forces, existing without discernible form, and wreaking emotional havoc upon its members, this representation of the family exists without symmetry or beauty.

Onlookers will be able to empathize with those who work with families; for as one gazes at Jacques Lipchitz' statue, it is difficult to discern where the problem began or what can be done to correct it. One thought is indelibly impressed upon the observer, however: This portrayal of the family as a grotesque institution bears no resemblance to its divinely ordained ideal.

BY-PRODUCTS OF PROGRESS

Caught up in the center of all this confusion is the wife and mother, who is now frequently also both homemaker and career woman.

A Bit of History Helps

Because many of the problems facing us as a society are of comparatively recent origin, it may help us to take a backward look and see where we have been.

Up to the 1940s, very few wives and mothers worked outside the home. Life was hard. Only a handful of household appliances were available. There were also fewer cars. Doing the washing, shopping for groceries, and cleaning the house took time—a great deal of time—and effort!

The war spurred industry into action. To aid the cause of freedom, women entered the job market where they were trained in a variety of skilled functions.

After the war, the question facing every industrial and commercial enterprise was, How may we make the most use of the skilled "man"-power available? Invention and innovation, marketing and research became the watchwords. Domestic appliances proliferated. Washing machines and vacuum cleaners were improved, clothes dryers became common in many homes, and cars of all shapes and sizes were manufactured. And education, which had been on the rise since the 1930s, promised a better way of life for all Americans.

With prosperity being enjoyed by an ever-increasing number of people, certain priorities began to fade from the scene. Their departure was almost imperceptible at first. *Historically, we can see that material possessions began to replace human values.* Ease and comfort began to supresede individual initiative and hard work. A commitment to Christian principles was replaced by ethical relativism and policies based on expediency.

For a while, the home continued as the center of American life. As pressures mounted, however, the centrifugal forces at work in society brought about an increase in feelings of frustration. Self-direction and self-fulfillment replaced the unity of the family. Divorce became more common. With the rise of divorce, we entered the era of single-parent families and "latchkey" children. Parental influence and example were now minimal, and permissiveness became normative.

It is no wonder, therefore, that Jacques Lipchitz portrays the modern American family as a grotesque, misshapen form that shocks our sensibilities. And many of us need to be shocked, for only out of this will come an awareness of what has happened in our lives.

Forgotten Priorities

How can we recover the richness, the satisfaction, and the reward of family living? What can we do to correct the self-centeredness of our generation, to restore our families to some degree of normalcy, and to begin to reverse the devastating effect our preoccupation with things has had upon our children?

As we grapple with this problem, let us see what we can learn from Claudia Procula, wife of Pontius Pilate.[1] Only one verse in the whole Bible is devoted to her. However, when this verse is carefully analyzed and correlated with historical facts derived from writers of antiquity, a most impressive picture begins to emerge.

In his pen portrait of Claudia, the great Scottish preacher, Dr. Alexander Whyte, wrote:

> Our men of natural science are able sometimes to reconstruct the shape and the size of a completely extinct species

from a single bone, or splinter of a bone, that has been quite accidentally dug out of the earth. And in something of the same way, Pilate's wife rises up before us out of a single sentence in Matthew's Gospel. We see the governor's wife only for a moment. We hear her only for a moment. But in the space of that short moment of time, she so impresses her sudden footprint on this page of this Gospel, that as long as this Gospel is read, this that Pilate's wife said and did that Passover morning shall be held in remembrance for a most honorable memorial of her.

Both Pilate and his wife, in Paul's words, were Gentiles in the flesh, being aliens from the commonwealth of Israel and strangers from the covenants of promise, having no hope, and without God in the world. Both Pilate and his wife were perfect heathens, as we would say. They were still at what we would call the pre-patriarchal period of divine revelation. They were still very much what Abraham himself was when God chose him, and spoke to him, and said to him, "Get thee out of thy country, and from thy kindred, and from thy father's house, unto a land that I will show thee." As regards many of the good things of this life: learning, civilization, refinement, and such like; the Roman governor and his gifted wife were very far advanced; but as regards what our Lord estimates to be the one thing needful for all men, they were not unlike Terah, and Nahor, and Abram . . . and still served other gods. Both Pilate and his wife were still at that stage in which God was wont to speak to men at sundry times and in divers manners; and, among other manners, in the manner of a dream.[2]

PRESENTING BOTH SIDES

At the time of our story, Pilate is procurator of the territories of Judea, Samaria, and Idumea. He is known to us historically because of the part he played in the trial and execution of Jesus Christ. At the height of the trial, "while he was sitting on the judgment seat, his wife sent [a message] to him saying, 'Have nothing to do with that righteous Man; for last night I suffered greatly in a dream because of him.'"

In this single sentence, we see . . .

- Claudia's strong convictions of right and wrong;
- Her love and concern for her husband and earnest desire to keep him from making a tragic mistake;
- Her independence of thought and action;
- Her discreet communication (for the Defendant is not named); and
- Her courage, for she knows that any communication to a judge while a trial is in progress is a serious and punishable offense.

What emerges from this verse is evidence of a woman whose commitments and priorities, wisdom and boldness of spirit give evidence of the singleness of purpose of her life. In addition, the message she sends to her husband—and her confidence that it will be received in the right spirit—indicates that a healthy level of communication characterizes their marriage.

Fixtures of Time

Claudia is the granddaughter of Augustus Caesar (the one whose census necessitated Joseph and Mary's journey to Bethlehem) and the daughter of Julia, whose immoral conduct raised eyebrows even in pagan Rome. Her home life has seen the tangled skein of intrigue and plots woven by her grandmother, Livia, as well as the degrading moral aberrations of the Empress Agrippina.

Something of the moral degeneracy of the times has been recorded for us by early Roman writers.[3] Seneca, for example, states that women began recording their age by the names of their husbands. Juvenal confirms this by citing the case of one woman who had had eight husbands in five years. Jerome declares that a case was known to him of a woman who had just married her twenty-third husband, and she was his twenty-first wife. Avarice, prostitution, and a complete disregard for human life permeated the society of their day.

Critical Difference

It is in such an atmosphere that Claudia marries the young and gallant Pontius Pilate. He is a member of the emperor's imperial staff and does not seem to be caught up in Rome's obsessions with sexual orgies, perverse games, and drunken behavior. As a member of the equestrian (upper middle-class) order, Pilate holds a coveted commission in the army. He has recently returned from active duty in Germany.

Claudia is probably in her early teens when she meets Pilate. She is doubtless fascinated by the stories he told of military campaigns against the Germanic tribes. She senses in him determination, character, and purpose—traits that, lamentably, will later develop into and be described by King Agrippa as "inflexibility, mercilessness and obstinacy."

Soon after Claudia has accepted Pilate's proposal of marriage, Pilate comes under the influence of Sejanus. Sejanus' star is rising in Rome's political firmament. He proves, however, to be treacherous and despotic. Under the guise of purging Rome of traitors who are disloyal to Tiberius, he has hundreds of people seized, imprisoned, and executed.

Claudia recognizes in Sejanus the kind of administrative skills needed in Rome at that time, but she must have deplored his abuse of the powers delegated to him by Tiberius. She must also have grown increasingly unhappy as she sees Pilate being drawn into the circle of his influence. Whatever her feelings—and we may be sure that she discussed her misgivings with Pilate—she manages to preserve her marriage and develop her relationship with her husband.

Facing a Troubled Future

With the degrading atmosphere of Rome exerting pressure on them, and with the political environment causing her increased concern, Claudia probably welcomes Pilate's announcement that he has applied for a political position. This will mean that before he can be elected to the Senate, he will have to have service overseas. In other words, they will have to leave Rome. Claudia knows that she will miss the sports, circuses, and some of the festive holidays, but to be away for the degeneracy of the Imperial City will be good for both of them.

Eager to advance the cause of her husband, Claudia may have tactfully tried to obtain Tiberius' help. He, however, is spending more and more of his time on the island of Capri. If he does recommend Pilate, the Senate probably feels indifferently toward the young equestrian, for they give him the least prestigious of all governorships: Judea, Samaria, and Idumea. There he will also be under the watchful eye of the powerful legate of Syria.[4]

The wives of Roman officials normally did not accompany their husbands on "foreign assignments." Tacitus, the Roman historian, records that about two years before Pilate was appointed to the Jewish provinces, this regulation was repealed. Of course, on the basis of precedent, Claudia could easily have remained in Rome. She, however, chooses to leave behind her the luxuries and comforts she has always known in order to accompany her husband to the despised land of the Jews.

Rising Woes

After making the long journey from the city of Rome to Caesarea on the eastern shores of the Mediterranean, Claudia and Pilate settle in Herod's summer palace. The azure sea and picturesque shoreline make up in beauty for what the country lacks in amenities and entertainment.

Some sections of the Christian church believe Claudia became increasingly interested in the religion of the Jews and was later a convert to Christianity. The Coptics also believe that Pilate came to faith in Christ, but not until after he had been recalled to Rome (A.D. 36). These traditions, though persistent, are not based upon verifiable facts.

What we may be sure of is that Claudia grieves over her husband's administrative blunders. He has probably picked up a dislike for the Jews from Sejanus. He also certainly resents his appointment to Judea, the most troublesome of all Rome's provinces. He lacks patience and feels that he can accomplish by force what his predecessors have failed to achieve through diplomacy. Claudia watches, therefore, as Pilate commits one political fiasco after another.[5] As far as the New Testament is concerned, these culminate in the trial and execution of Jesus Christ.

HONEST AND TENDER

No woman likes to be the wife of a man who is a failure. She likes to be able to look up to, respect, and admire her husband.

As best she can, Claudia tries to be supportive of Pilate and temper his hot impetuosity. But this is not easy, for the leaders of the Jews are resentful of Rome's domination of them and their nation.

Eight difficult years pass. At best a "cold war" prevails between Pilate and the Jews. The taxes are sent regularly to Rome, but the Jewish penchant for reporting Pilate's misdeeds to Tiberius has all but ruined his prospects of promotion.

As the months pass, the time of the Jewish Passover approaches. Claudia has learned that this festival commemorates the liberation of the Hebrews as a nation from the might of the Egyptian pharaoh. Nationalism runs high at this time of year. In order to be on hand should trouble break out, Pilate and Claudia journey to Jerusalem. There they occupy Herod's old palace. There, too, they will have to spend one evening entertaining King Agrippa and his wife, Herodias. They do not care for either of them, but governors and their wives are expected to engage in diplomacy and not allow their private feelings to interfere with official business.

The Real Rabble-Rousers

It is toward evening on Thursday that the Jewish leaders approach Pilate with a request for soldiers to help them apprehend a dangerous criminal. They are obsequious in their courtesy, and this makes Claudia suspicious.

Claudia, of course, has heard of Jesus of Nazareth. All Galilee and Judea have been talking about Him. Rumor even has it that He raised a dead man to life in a village only a few miles from Jerusalem (John 11). Furthermore, on Sunday, He had caused a commotion in Jerusalem itself. From reports she has received, He apparently rode into the city on a donkey, with the people clamoring something about Him being a king, the "Son of David" (see Mark 11:9–10).

All of these things cause her growing anxiety. She can tell

that her husband is reaching a point of exasperation. She knows that, above all else, he must avoid more trouble with the Jews.

Anguish and Confusion

Early Friday morning, someone bangs on the door of the palace. Claudia wishes that one of the servants would answer and tell whoever it is to go away. The banging stops as she hears the bolts of the door being opened. There is the sound of voices. A note of urgency is communicated by the tone. Then there is silence. She hears the sound of someone coming up the stairs. The door leading into an adjoining room opens and someone enters. Then there is a knock on their bedroom door. Pilate has been awakened by the commotion. He grumbles his disgust, rises, and pulls on a robe. With ill-disguised annoyance, he shuffles across the floor and enters the outer room where a centurion is waiting to speak to him.

It had been a late night for Claudia and Pilate. They had entertained Agrippa and Herodias, one of those boring, but necessary, social functions. Claudia found Herodias to be even more opinionated than ever. From the conversation, she learned that Herodias had finally persuaded her husband to get rid of a prophet who had been biasing the minds of the people against her (Matt. 14:3–11).

With the dinner finally over, it seemed to Claudia as if they had only just gotten into bed when there was this disturbance downstairs. She can hear muffled voices in the other room. Pilate dismisses the centurion and returns to the bedroom. He begins to dress.

"The Jews," he confides, "have apprehended their 'revolutionary' and they want me to pronounce sentence now so that they can have Him executed *before* the Passover begins at sundown."

Claudia drifts off into sleep again. She has no means of knowing that the man on trial before her husband is the Prophet from Galilee about whom she has heard so much.

During the time Jesus is on trial before Pilate, Claudia has a dream. It lasts for only a moment, but it alarms her so much that she awakens from a sound sleep. Her heart is pounding. She is afraid.

Dressing hastily, she makes her way to the Praetorium. She can see her husband. From his attitude and tone of voice, she can sense that he is losing patience with the Jews. He is angry. The high priests, who are laying charges against the accused, are plainly unscrupulous. They keep on changing their charge (Matt. 27:12–13).

Claudia senses Pilate's mounting desperation as he seeks to dismiss the case. Finally, in a friendly gesture, he offers to release either Barabbas or Jesus to them. There is a lull while the Jews outside deliberate with their other Sanhedrinists over Pilate's offer. Claudia takes advantage of this brief interlude to send her husband a message: *"Do not have anything to do with this righteous man; for I have suffered greatly in a dream because of Him."* It is a bold step for her to take.

Courage Amid Confusion

Roman jurisprudence had developed an orderly legal system permitting a surprisingly equitable administration of justice. It forbade the wives of magistrates to meddle in courtroom affairs. If a wife or any member of a Roman official's family interfered in any way while he was presiding over a case, they were automatically guilty of contempt of court. Their punishment was severe, ranging from a heavy fine to imprisonment.

Pilate is jolted by Claudia's message. He then tries by all the expedients of his profession to secure the release of

Jesus. In the end, when the Pharisees resort to threats and intimidation, he capitulates (John 19:12). *"Ibis ad crucem,"* he finally says to the centurion. And Jesus is led away to be crucified.

NO "I TOLD YOU SO'S"

Pilate must have returned to their bedroom a sad man. He had lost another round in his dealings with the Jews.

In a few years, what he feared most would happen. He would be recalled by Tiberius to answer charges brought against him by the high priests and rulers of the people. Then, stripped of all rank, he would be sent into exile.

Claudia, of course, could remain in Rome. Their society would expect her to divorce Pilate and marry a senator or some other public figure whose political fortunes were better than Pilate's.

Claudia, so historians tell us, remained by Pilate's side. She shared with him whatever life meted out to them. Loyalty, therefore, must also be numbered among her virtues.

THE ROCKY ROAD TO MARITAL HARMONY

Of importance to us, as we reflect upon Claudia's social milieu and life with Pilate, is, What did she contribute to their union? How did she maintain their relationship when there were so many divisive factors at work that could easily have destroyed their marriage?

We have already seen that Claudia was a woman of rare courage and conviction. She was committed to preserving their relationship. She was also supportive of her husband. The Bible affirms all this. It also lays stress upon the high level of communication that evidently characterized their marriage. There was open and free interaction. *Claudia knew she could share her innermost thoughts and feelings with her husband, and she had the confidence that he would receive her words in the same spirit in which they were sent.*

Not many marriages can boast such a spirit of mutual acceptance, love, and understanding.

Good communication is the key to a healthy marriage.[6] Good communication, however, is hindered by attitudes of *hostility, superiority, selfishness, dogmatism, insensitivity, and censure.* These may all be communicated on an unconscious, feeling level. If you look again at Claudia's message to Pilate—short, but giving evidence of her fears for his well-being—you will find an absence of these negative elements.

Good communication thrives in an atmosphere of acceptance and understanding. To develop the ability to communicate effectively, we need to master the art of empathy. This takes place as we learn how to listen to what our spouse is saying. Pilate did. He received Claudia's message and tried all the harder to release Jesus. The more empathic we each become, the deeper will be the level of our understanding.

In the process of developing good communication, we need to recognize and admit our feelings as a part of the process of becoming sensitive to the feelings of others. This will prepare us to understand the dynamics of love in which we share our feelings in an atmosphere of mutual acceptance.

In an earlier chapter, we mentioned the book by Sheldon Vanauken entitled *A Severe Mercy*. Such was the level of communication between Van and Davy that their friends were astounded by it.

Dr. Vanauken writes:

We sought closeness through sharing in order to keep in-loveness. . . . we could always talk together. . . . Sometimes we had fights. . . . [these] always came when we got a little out of harmony with each other.[7]

However, as Van and Davy shared more and more of themselves, their ability to communicate developed. There existed between them a spirit of total trust.

Van goes on to tell of an incident that took place one evening while they were entertaining some friends. One of those present noticed Davy look at some candles on the mantlepiece. A few moments later, Van rose to light them. He had subconsciously picked up on Davy's expressed desire.

What Pilate and Claudia achieved, and what Sheldon and Davy Vanauken developed, is possible for us as well. *The key to unlocking the secrets of a happy marriage lies, initially, in our learning how to listen with feeling for the other person and with an understanding of their needs and desires.* Once we have learned how to listen to each other, we can begin to develop true unity in our relationship.

Interaction

1. All that was degrading in the ancient Roman empire is present in our society. Pilate and Claudia had to work hard to build and then maintain their marriage. What do you think were some of the corrosive elements threatening their relationship? How do you think they established a strong, durable marriage?

2. Claudia could have kept silent while Pilate was in the Judgment Hall. She did not. Why? How do you think she handled the outcome of the trial?

3. Claudia appears on the pages of the Gospels in much the same light as the wife of an upward-moving business executive today. What does she have in common with her twentieth-century counterpart? Claudia contributed to Pilate's public and private life—assisting with the former and enriching the latter. How do you think she was able to do this without giving the appearance of being "the power behind the throne"?

Claudia's communication to Pilate shows that she was a woman of independent thought and action, concerned for her husband, yet believing that Jesus, the Preacher from Nazareth, was a righteous man. How was she able to give expression to her convictions without causing Pilate to feel that she was meddling in his affairs? (Note: There is no evidence of Pilate's loss of face following his receipt of her message, but only a record of the fact that he tried harder to release Jesus.)

5. Communication is a key element in developing unity between a husband and wife, or between parents and their children. Discuss some of the barriers that clog up the channels of good communication. Then consider some of the positive ways in which good communication may be attained and maintained. (Note: Healthy communication between a husband and wife is essential *before* any effective, lasting communication can be established between parents and their children.)

12

Ahead of
Their Time

*Next to Charles Wordsworth's deep religious faith, the
most blessed influence on his life was undoubtedly that
of his devoted wife who was never far distant, and who
was completely one with him.* —J. H. Overton
and E. Wordsworth

We were visiting some friends one evening when our host
remarked, "I do not believe that the Bible is a valid guide for
life on earth."

After those who were present had had time to recover
from their initial surprise, our host continued by saying, "In
fact, I do not believe that it has the answers to any of the
dilemmas mankind has faced in this or any other age. In my
profession as a practicing psychologist, I find too many people grappling with problems that are not discussed in the
Bible. I believe that God has given us minds with which to
think and reason and that with our minds He expects us to
solve our own problems."

LIVELY DISCUSSION

Our host's statement may appear at first to be quite radical, particularly when compared to the doctrinal beliefs of
the evangelical church to which he belongs. However, the

majority of the men in his home that evening were sympathetic with his views.

Of course, a lively discussion ensued. The wives participated. Some of them had experienced firsthand the predicaments being described by their husbands and did not hesitate to point out how, by following the teaching of Scripture, they had been able to handle successfully these difficult situations.

As the discussion went back and forth, illustrations of the kinds of problems supposedly not dealt with in the Bible, but presently impacting society, were mentioned. These included modern methods of birth control making possible a large number of working wives, also single parent families, the decline of the American "hero," permissiveness in the home, the virtual disappearance of the local church as a vital force in the community, and the emergence of male passivity, permitting the rise of a matriarchy.

As timely as these issues are, we believe that the Bible does contain the answer to the dilemmas facing us today. Through direct precepts as well as through biographies, illustration is added to instruction, and when all the data is merged, we have examples as well as exhortations in the Bible about what our lives and homes should be like.[1]

The point to be borne in mind is that the *better we know our Bibles, the easier it is for us to relate its teaching to our particular situation.*

For example, some of the questions raised by our host that evening find their answer in a study of the lives of Priscilla and Aquila. However, because the information concerning this couple is scattered throughout the Book of Acts and the epistles of Paul, we will need to draw the threads together before we will be able to learn from their example.

THE LONG HAND OF HISTORY

The Proud City

In Rome, Tiberius (who had recalled Pilate from Judea) had died. He had been succeeded by Caligula, whose mad rule of only four years had plunged the once-proud city into chaos. Following Caligula's assassination, the weak and foolish Claudius was made emperor (A.D. 41).[2] The Senate approved of his appointment because they felt he would be easier to control than his predecessor had been. It is during the reign of Claudius that the lives of two people, Aquila and Priscilla, are drawn together.

Aquila is from Pontus on the southern shores of the Black Sea. He is a Jew. We have no means of knowing how old he is at the time he journeys to Rome. In keeping with the traditions of the Jews, however, he has been taught a trade. In addition to his profession, he is also a tentmaker.

Whether Aquila became a believer in the Lord Jesus while in Pontus (1 Peter 1:1–2) or came to faith in Christ as a result of the influence of Christians in Rome cannot be determined from the biblical text. We do know that while in Rome he meets and marries a young woman named Prisca.

Prisca is a Gentile Christian, and her union with Aquila demonstrates the breaking down of the barrier that has previously separated Jews and Gentiles (Eph. 2:14–16). Such is the winsomeness and charm of Prisca's personality, that everyone calls her by the diminutive form of her name, Priscilla.

Reading Between the Lines

Aquila and Priscilla are mentioned six times in God's Word. *They always appear together.* Apparently, neither did anything without the other. *Theirs is a unity that transcends the expected and the ordinary.*

Dr. Arthur C. McGiffert, in *The Apostolic Age*, has pointed out that: "[Aquila and Priscilla] furnish the most beautiful example known to us in the apostolic age of the power for good that can be exerted by a husband and wife working in unison for the advancement of the gospel."[3]

Four times in the Scriptures, Priscilla's name appears first. This is unusual. In the Bible, the order is usually the man first, as in Adam and Eve, Abraham and Sarah, Samson and Delilah. This has led some writers to speculate that Priscilla was of noble birth. Others believe that she was more outgoing than her husband. The Lutheran commentator, Dr. R. C. H. Lenski, says quite emphatically, "In character, ability, devotion she excelled her husband so evidently that her name had to precede his."[4] Whatever Priscilla's attainments or heritage, she never allows them to come between her and her husband.

Troubled Future

In Rome after their marriage, all goes well for a while. Then, in A.D. 50, when the Jews cause one disturbance too many, Claudius commands them to leave the Imperial City (Acts 18:2).[5] This includes Aquila. It does not involve Priscilla, for she is a Roman. Priscilla, however, willingly shares her husband's exile, and they sail for Corinth on the isthmus of Greece.

Being a tentmaker, Aquila believes that he can make a good living in Corinth, for the city controls trade from both north and south, east and west.

Dr. William Barclay explains the geographic situation of Corinth as well as the moral degradation of that city:

> A glance at the map of Greece will show that Corinth was made for greatness. The southern part of Greece is very

nearly an island. On the west the Saronic Gulf deeply indents the land, and on the east the Corinthian Gulf. All that is left to join the two parts of Greece together is a little isthmus only four miles across. On that narrow neck of land, Corinth stands. Such a position made it inevitable that Corinth should be one of the greatest trading and commercial centers of the ancient world . . .

But there was another side to Corinth. She had a reputation for commercial prosperity, but she was also a by-word for evil and immoral living. The very word *korinthiazesthai*, to live like a Corinthian, had become a part of the Greek language, and it meant to live with drunken and immoral debauchery. The word has actually penetrated to the English language, and, in Regency times, a Corinthian was one of the wealthy young bucks who lived in reckless and in riotous living. Aelian, the late Greek writer, tells us that if ever a Corinthian was shown upon the stage in a Greek play, he was shown drunk. The very name Corinth was synonymous with debauchery. But in the old days there was one source of evil in Corinth that was known all over the civilized world. Above the isthmus there towered the hill of the Acropolis, and on it there stood the great temple of Aphrodite, the goddess of love. To that temple there were attached one thousand priestesses who were sacred prostitutes, and at evening time they descended from the Acropolis and plied their trade upon the streets of Corinth, until it became a Greek proverb, "It is not every man who can afford a journey to Corinth." In addition to these cruder sins, there flourished in Corinth far more recondite vices, which had come in with the traders and the sailors from the ends of the earth, until Corinth became not only a synonym for wealth and luxury, drunkenness, and debauchery, but also for filth.[6]

Aquila and Priscilla come to Corinth never realizing tnat at the same time the Lord is bringing them, through Thessalonica, Berea, and Athens, a man who will need their friendship and change the course of their lives.

BETTER THAN EXPECTED

Paul, the man whom God is bringing to Corinth, has had a most disappointing experience in Athens. He has ministered there with only marginal success. He has felt his aloneness (1 Thess. 3:1) and, following the rejection of his ministry, has decided to move on to Corinth. By the time he arrives there, however, he is penniless.

In keeping with the tradition of the Jews, his father had taught him a trade (Acts 18:3). This he had acquired in addition to being educated in philosophy at the University of Tarsus and in theology at the feet of Gamaliel at the "seminary" in Jerusalem.

Paul, therefore, seeks out those whose trade is similar to his own. He does so with the hope of finding work. His inquiries lead him to a little shop recently opened by Aquila and Priscilla. When they find that Paul, in addition to being a tentmaker like themselves, is a Christian, this couple not only employ him, but they welcome him into their home as well.

Paul remains in Corinth for eighteen months. He begins his ministry among the Jews by reasoning with them in their synagogue. Later, he uses the house of Titius as the center of his operations.

In the evenings, however, Paul returns to the home of Aquila and Priscilla and spends his time with them. As a result, this couple grow in their faith. They soon come to a place in their experience where they can begin teaching others. And in what better place can they advance the cause of Christ than in their home (Acts 18:24, 26; Rom. 16:3, 5; 1 Cor. 16:19)?

IT'S NEVER BEEN DONE
THIS WAY BEFORE

Following a very successful ministry in Corinth, Paul decides to return to Jerusalem via Ephesus. He desires to start a work for the Lord in the "City of Diana" on his next missionary journey. Not wishing to repeat his experience at Athens, he asks Priscilla and Aquila to accompany him. His plan is to leave them in Ephesus. There they are to start what we today would call a "home Bible class." Then, when he returns, there will be a nucleus of believers among whom he can work. Priscilla and Aquila agree to Paul's plan. In Ephesus they continue to ply their trade while using their home for spreading the gospel.

Base of Operations

Ephesus has been called "The Vanity Fair of the Ancient World," the "Supreme Metropolis of Asia," and the "Queen of Ionia." It was once the proud capital of that region and served as the chief harbor of proconsular Asia. Because it was also situated at the mouth of the River Cayster with three main roads converging on its shores, Ephesus was also a city of great commercial importance.

The Romans had made Ephesus a "free city." This meant that they had been granted the right of self-government and did not have to put up with a garrison of Roman soldiers quartered within their walls. In addition, the Ephesians were permitted to dispense justice. This meant that they became the seat of magisterial authority with plaintiffs coming to them, rather than their citizens having to go elsewhere.

The greatest attraction in Ephesus, however, was the famed Temple of Diana (or in Greek, Artemis). It was one of the seven wonders of the ancient world. The Greeks had coined a saying that the "sun sees nothing finer in its course than Diana's temple." Attached to the temple were thousands of priestesses known as *Melissae*. They served the same purpose as the female devotees of the temples in Corinth.

In addition, Ephesus was known for its famous library and the sale of the *Ephesian Letters*—spells written in an indecipherable script. They could be purchased and would bring to the buyer his or her heart's desire.

Paul brings Priscilla and Aquila to Ephesus; here they are to begin to spread the message of God's saving grace. A reading of Acts 19:18–20 provides further evidence of the widespread practice of the "black arts" in Ephesus and illustrates how hard it must have been for this couple to evangelize their neighborhood.

Winning Ways

It is while Priscilla and Aquila are in Ephesus that Apollos, a Jew from Alexandria in Egypt, comes to the city. He is on a preaching mission throughout that region.

This godly couple, who have benefited from the instruction of Paul while in Corinth, detect that something is missing from the content of Apollos' messages. They, therefore, "take him aside" into the privacy of their home and explain to him the "way of God" with greater accuracy.

From what is recorded, it appears as if Priscilla took the initiative (Acts 18:25). Dr. D. Edmond Hiebert writes:

> The order of their names here implies that Priscilla led in their ministry to Apollos. . . . "She was by nature more gifted and able than her husband. . . . Aquila seems to have been a gentle, quiet soul, genuine in his unobtrusive way." It is an eloquent testimony to Priscilla and Aquila's tact and graciousness that [Apollos], this university graduate and noted rabbi,

readily received their instruction. The ministry they rendered in the privacy of their home proved to be a great boon to the cause of Christ.[7]

Return of the Apostle

When Paul returns to Ephesus several years later, he finds a nucleus of believers in the city. As is his custom, he begins by ministering in the synagogue. When the Jews reject his words, he moves to the school of Tyrannus. He teaches there for two years. Such is the impact of his ministry that "all who live in Asia hear the world of the Lord" (Acts 19:10).

This is a most remarkable statement. But where did the first students come from? There is no record of an influx of new believers from his ministry in the synagogue. The answer seems to lie in the fact that those whom Paul sent out to evangelize the interior of Asia had been won to Christ by Priscilla and Aquila (1 Cor. 16:19. This letter to the Corinthians was written from Ephesus).

Caught in Passing

Some years later (A.D. 58), Paul again visits Corinth. He learns that Phoebe is journeying to Rome. He decides to write the believers in that city and entrust the letter to this gentle woman. In doing so, he closes by sending greetings to some friends who are living in the imperial city. He writes:

"Greet Prisca [the more formal form of Priscilla's name, befitting someone of noble birth] and Aquila, *my fellowworkers in Christ Jesus . . . and the church that is in their house*" (Rom. 16:3, 5).

But when had Priscilla and Aquila returned to Rome? The last we knew was that Jews had been driven out by Claudius' edict. In A.D. 54, Nero had succeeded Claudius.

From Romans, chapter 16, it seems evident that the ban preventing Jews from living amid Rome's seven hills had been lifted. Priscilla and Aquila were, therefore, free to return to the Imperial City.

Earlier, however, while in Ephesus, Paul had expressed his desire to visit Rome (Acts 19:21; Rom. 1:9–10, 13). Did Paul privately communicate his desire to Priscilla and Aquila and request them to go to Rome ahead of him? We do not know. What is certain is that, for some reason or other, Priscilla and Aquila return to Italy. There they begin witnessing to their friends and neighbors. In time, they have a group of believers meeting in their home.

The Autumn of Life

From the Book of Acts we know that Paul finally reaches Rome . . . in chains (Acts 20:22–23; 21:3–5, 10–14; 25:6–12; 28:16ff.). He spends two years under a form of house arrest (Acts 28:30–31), ministering to all who visit him. He is then released.

Exactly where Paul preaches during his few years of freedom is uncertain. Nero, however, is not kindly disposed toward Christians. Apparently Priscilla and Aquila feel it is wise to leave Rome, for when Paul is again imprisoned, he writes to Timothy in Ephesus. In concluding his letter, he sends greetings to "Prisca and Aquila and the house of Onesiphorus" (2 Tim. 4:19). Apparently, even in their declining years, they were active in the work they had helped establish.

JUSTIFIABLE PRAISE

Having reviewed in kaleidoscopic form the activities of Priscilla and Aquila, we are now able to reflect on the chief reason for the success of their marriage. We find this to lie in their *unity*. They are always mentioned together. The differences in their social rank and ethnic backgrounds could have made real unity difficult. How, then, are we to explain their success?

The key seems to lie in the person of Priscilla. She was in a position whereby she could be either the greatest blessing or the greatest hindrance in Aquila's life.

Appropriate Priorities

In unravelling the secret of their success, we find first of all that Priscilla and Aquila were each committed to marrying a Christian. Priscilla, being probably of noble birth, would have had many suitors. She could have married someone rich and famous. She chose instead to marry a person who shared the same beliefs she had. And Aquila, being a Jew, would naturally have had pressure brought to bear upon him to marry someone from his own race. Instead, we find him marrying a Gentile who is a Christian.

Once married, Aquila and Priscilla commit themselves to each other. Aquila was not of Priscilla's social level and had not benefited from the same fine education that she had received. These differences, however, were regarded as unimportant. What they were in Christ *was* important. Priscilla, therefore, dedicated herself to being all that a Christian wife should be.

Priscilla's loyalty to Aquila was tested when Claudius expelled all Jews from Rome. She willingly left family and friends and went to live in a different country where she had to speak Greek (not the cultured and refined Latin of Roman society) in order that she might be with her husband.

From a consideration of these facts, we may safely conclude that the marriage of Priscilla and Aquila was characterized by an uncommon unity.

Entertaining God's Messenger

After settling in Corinth, Priscilla, who had probably been reared in a home with servants who did the menial chores, worked with Aquila in making tents. Theirs was not a "dual-career" family. They rented a shop that probably had living quarters either at the back of or above the store. This humble abode was their new home.

It was to their shop that they welcomed the apostle Paul as a partner and permanent houseguest (Heb. 13:2).

They worked along with Paul as he began his ministry in the city, rejoiced with him as people were saved, and "sat at his feet" as he taught them in the evenings after the work of the day was done (Acts 18:4). During the months spent in Corinth, Aquila and Priscilla grew in the faith. They proved so helpful to Paul, that he invited them to do some "church-planting" in Ephesus.

Many women find it difficult to become involved in their church activities because they happen to work. The meetings, it seems, are always at the wrong time. Visitation teams are organized during the day, while they are at the office. Fellowship groups meet in the mornings, when they are at work; and prayer meetings at night seem to conflict with their responsibilities to their families.

It is encouraging to see from Priscilla's example that a working wife can have a ministry. She can extend hospitality to those in need and engage in "home Bible classes"—all within her home. Increased attention, therefore, needs to be given to the place of the home in the outreach of the church.

Unusual Ministry

When Aquila and Priscilla were left behind in Ephesus by Paul, they probably worshiped in the local synagogue. It was there one Sabbath that a traveling rabbi ministered to those in attendance. He gave evidence of being a genuine believer in "the Way," but his theology was faulty. He did not have what we would call today a clearly defined Christology. Now, how do you tell a learned *rabbi* that his theology is weak? Priscilla and Aquila did.

Of course, this was a golden opportunity for Priscilla to display her learning. After all, she had been educated in Rome and had received her "graduate training" in theology under the apostle Paul. With her classical background in rhetoric and philosophy, she was more than a match for any man in a discussion.

An attitude of assured superiority, however, cannot be concealed. It manifests itself in subtle ways. Apollos would not have been insensitive to the fact that this Gentile woman knew more about Christ and the Scriptures than he did. How, then, was Priscilla able to instruct him in the truths about Christ's person and work (Acts 18:24–28)?

Apparently, Priscilla did not feel the need to compete with Apollos; neither did she feel the need to display her abilities. Many years earlier, her winsomeness had endeared her to those in Rome. Her less accomplished husband felt comfortable in her presence. Paul was fond of her (using her familiar name, not the formal Prisca). *She was content to be a woman and did not see the need to be in competition with any man.* And with these issues settled, she could concentrate on being helpful.

Contentment is a rare gift. The different liberation movements that have arisen in recent decades have stressed the need for women to vie with men for the top positions in their companies, for bigger and better benefits, and for greater and grander status symbols. In the process, women have become discontented and have lost that which is of the utmost importance to them, their femininity.

This process has been going on long enough for us to be able to observe its effects. Dr. Martina Horner, President of Radcliffe College, following extensive research, wrote about the internal conflict—the fear of success or fear of failure— being experienced by many women who no longer have a clearly defined identity:

> Many women fear success; they worry about the negative consequences that can arise from moving ahead in a career. These anxieties can inhibit them.
>
> The sources of the fear differ for each individual and can change at various points in life. Some women, especially those who came of age in the 1950s and '60s, feared that if they pursued a career, society would react against them, they wouldn't get married, and they would be viewed as unattractive and unfeminine. For others, the anxiety is more fundamental, growing out of fear of outperforming people they care about, such as husbands and boyfriends . . .
>
> Today, some women who pursued careers are saying that the price of success is too high. They are beginning to want to have children and deeper relationships. They viewed the career route as the primary source of their hopes and now are questioning that decision. This is in contrast to women who came of age in the '50s and '60s and sought the rewards of home and family.[8]

How interesting to read this description and to compare it to Priscilla, a woman who was happy, fulfilled, and influential. In her supportive role, she was able to assist her husband, extend hospitality to Paul, nurture the new Christians, and counsel Apollos. And in the process, she enjoyed that inner sense of satisfaction that all women seek and few can describe.

Supreme Praise

The effectiveness of the lives of Aquila and Priscilla may be gauged from the apostle Paul's words when he spoke of them as his "fellow-workers," whose lives had benefited "all the churches of the Gentiles" (Rom. 16:3–4).

Dr. A. T. Robertson comments on this statement as follows:

> Priscilla and Aquila were Paul's "fellow-workers in Christ Jesus" whether in Corinth, Ephesus or Rome. Paul is grateful for them, but many others also feel the same way, "all the churches of the Gentiles" in fact. Here we catch a glimpse of the missionary zeal of this couple. They were known and loved, Paul says, through Gentile Christendom. They were great travellers, but they took Christ with them wherever they went. Like Abraham of old, they set up an altar to the Lord [of worship and witness] in every city. . . . They were rich in their friends and in their service.[9]

As we reflect upon the life of this couple, we find that they illustrate for us the unity and usefulness, personal fulfillment and happiness we all desire. They withstood the onslaught of worldliness in each city in which they lived, extended hospitality to those in need, established house-churches, and ministered to others whenever the opportunity presented itself. The result was that they, together, led rewarding, productive lives. Their life together serves as a model of what ours may become.

Interaction

1. What are the most common problems—emotional, physical, psychological, spiritual—facing working wives today?

a. Make a list of these and discuss them together. How do these problems impact relationships within the home?

b. Those who have read A. C. Clarke's book *2001* or Toffler's *The Third Wave*, along with other works dealing with life fifteen to twenty years from now, will have noticed that these popularizers of conditions in the twenty-first century have predicted the demise of many of this country's larger corporations. They believe that the future will see a return to a form of private enterprise with men being the primary breadwinners (possibly working out of their homes or else in a store) and being assisted by their wives. Assuming this to be a possibility, what does the story of Priscilla and Aquila teach us about life's values as well as about service in the cause of Christ?

2. Re-create in your mind the lives and circumstances of Aquila and Priscilla in each place in which they lived. What problems may they have faced as Priscilla began working? From what we know of this couple, how do you think they would have handled these tensions?

3. Hospitality is encouraged in both the Old and the New Testaments (Gen. 18:1–8; 19:1–3; 24:25, 31–33; Lev. 19:34; Job 31:32; Luke 14:12–14; Rom. 12:13; Titus 1:8; Heb. 13:2; 1 Peter 4:9). Why?

4. Some people will attend Bible study in a home who would not attend a formal service in a church. Open discussion of issues of mutual interest can lead to a consideration of the Bible's teaching on the subject under consideration. Why have "cottage meetings" (as they were once called) or "home Bible classes" proved so successful?

5. Dr. Francis Schaeffer, in *The Church at the End of the Twentieth Century*, believes that by the year 2000 "house-churches" will again be the tradition among evangelical, theologically conservative Christians. What may be some of the advantages of this? Are there any disadvantages? If this does come about in the way Dr. Schaeffer describes, how will it affect your present lifestyle?

13

Love
Comes Softly

As a man beholds the woman,
As the woman sees the man,
Curiously they note each other,
As each other only can.
Never can the man divest her
Of that wondrous charm of sex;
Ever must she, dreaming of him,
That same mystic charm annex.
—Bryan Waller Procter

Among our friends are a number of publishers. These include editors of magazines as well as producers of books. Some of the stories they have told us of letters received in their offices provide an interesting commentary on people's attitudes.

For example, one month one of our friends approved a cover photo portraying a young husband and his pregnant wife walking together by the sea. It was a special issue for parents, the picture being designed to emphasize the importance of preparing for one's parental obligations.

This picture aroused a storm of protest. Letters were received in the editorial office expressing, in the strongest terms, the moral indignation of the writers. The picture, some of the correspondents felt, was "suggestive," and a few even went on to say that if this ever happened again they would cancel their subscription.

Another publisher told us of the angry responses he received when his company published a book on Genesis as a part of their Sunday school curriculum material. It was designed for young adults. In dealing with God's creation of Adam and the making of Eve, the author stated that God was the originator of sex. He went on to say that sex within the bounds of marriage was a beautiful expression of the love of the couple and symbolized their unity. Among those who wrote protesting the statement was a woman who claimed that intimacy between a man and a woman is "carnal knowledge," and that God could not be the originator of anything carnal.

Attitudes such as these have a devastating effect upon one's marriage as well as upon one's children. Husbands whom we have talked to at family camps and in our home have shared with us their sexual frustrations. Many of them have complained that their wives have a negative attitude toward intimacy. At best, they are "passive" or "just lie there" while their husbands make love to them, or they silently convey the message that "I endure this (sexual intercourse) only because I love you."

Wives, however, also have their frustrations. Because their husbands are unsure of themselves, they seldom give thought as to how their wives feel. In some cases, foreplay is virtually absent. One wife describes her husband's idea of making love in terms of her emotional and physical pain. Her husband, it appears, was in the habit of commencing intercourse with intromission. Three to five minutes later he would ejaculate, withdraw, give her a brief kiss, and roll over and go to sleep.

AN ANCIENT TESTIMONY

It might surprise us at first to realize that God, in His infinite wisdom, has included a "marriage manual" in the Bible. We refer, of course, to the Song of Solomon. This book contains the reflections of Solomon's *bride* on her marriage.

The book is written in the form of a play. For this reason, it is best to read it in a version of the Bible that describes the various actors and their parts. We recommend the *Ryrie Study Bible* or some other comparable work. The Song of Solomon does not follow a chronological sequence, but is rather a series of vignettes dealing with the courtship, marriage, and adjustments that Solomon and his bride had to make.

An Understanding of Love

There are various ways in which we can refer to the intimacies of marriage. Doctors use the antiseptic terminology of their profession. Purveyors of pornography and the publishers of cheap novels use the language of their trade. In reading Solomon's song, however, we find that God inspired him to use poetic symbols.[1]

As we consider this ancient love song, we find that, because of its explicit references to lovemaking, the Jewish rabbis would not allow a young man to read it until he was thirty. They rightly understood this song as designed by God to give its readers an appreciation of conjugal romance. They interpreted it as the glorification of the bliss of wedded life. It is no wonder, therefore, that in their culture, marriage represented the very highest, fullest, deepest, and most satisfying of all relationships. And so it should be.

In the course of time, however, the rabbis became embarrassed by their own interpretation and when Greek allegorism spread across the civilized world, they allegorized the Song of Solomon to represent God's love for Israel. This paved the way for the Christian church to see in it Christ's love for the Church. Certain verses (Song 1:13; 2:6; 3:4; and others), however, are impossible to explain in this way. It is, therefore, preferable to follow the normal method of interpretation and to understand the metaphors, symbols, and figures of speech in terms of the cultural background of the times.

LOVE IS NOT CARNAL

The story concerns a young Shulamite woman who lives in the north country, in the mountain district of Ephraim. She is from Shunem, a village near Baal-hamon where Solomon has a vineyard (Song 8:11).

It appears, from the way in which she describes her family (see 1:6), that her mother has been twice widowed. No mention is made of her father. Instead, her "mother's sons" (not "my brothers") are running the small farm. They resent her and make her do all the hard work, so much so that she has no time for herself ("my own vineyard," that is, my personal appearance, "I have not been able to care for" [1:6–7]).

The Mood of Spring

One day, as the Shulamite is busy either pasturing her brothers' flock or working in the vineyard, a handsome stranger passes by. He is dressed as a shepherd. Perhaps they exchange a greeting. They are attracted to each other, and she inquires where he is allowing his flock to feed (1:7).

The relationship of the "shepherd" and the Shulamite begins to ripen into love (1:2–4). There are times when they are happy in each other's arms, and there are times when, in the exuberance of youth, they playfully chase each other through the forests or fields.

He visits her as often as he can, and she begins to look forward to his calls (2:8–9).

One day the Shulamite learns that her "shepherd-lover" is really Solomon, the king. He proposes to her, but she is unsure of herself (2:10–13). She considers what marriage to him and life in the big city will mean to their relationship. He coaxes her, then leaves (v. 14).

Being a young woman, the Shulamite has probably shared her feelings toward her "shepherd" with her mother and friends. However, when she tells them that he is the king, they probably counsel her to forget her Cinderella-like romance. She becomes despondent, as they tell her that he will never return for her; she tries to reassure herself (2:16). She earnestly longs for his return (v. 17). Such is her anxiety, that it disturbs her sleep (3:1–4). She dreams of searching for him. When she finds him, she embraces him and brings him into her mother's house.

Then her dream ends. The next day is the same as the one before. Her beloved is not there. Perhaps he has forgotten her. Perhaps he will not come after all.

Love's Enduring Promise

One day, however, when the Shulamite has almost given up hope of ever seeing her beloved again, a cloud of dust is seen rising into the sky (3:6–11). It causes a commotion in Shunem, for it can either herald an invading army (in which case they should run for their lives), or it may be Israel's army marching into battle. In either case, the prospects are foreboding.

As the cause of the cloud of dust draws nearer, soldiers are seen. Then a sedan chair. The people begin to relax. It is probably some high official enroute to Megiddo to gather more taxes.

To everyone's surprise, the procession stops outside the Shulamite's home. Solomon has sent for his beloved; he has not forgotten her.

With royal pomp, the Shulamite is brought to Jerusalem. She is then taken to the palace where Solomon greets her and brings her into his personal chambers (1:4). There his maids take off her farm clothes and prepare her for the wedding (vv. 5–6).

AT LAST . . . TOGETHER

A lavish banquet is given to honor Solomon's new bride. The happy couple recline on couches facing a table on which the food has been placed. The guests do the same on couches all around the hall. The king and his beautiful shepherdess are together at last, and they engage in tender, loving conversation (1:9–2:6).

A careful consideration of these verses gives us a clear idea as to the attitude of Solomon and the Shulamite about themselves and each other. Solomon assures his young bride of her beauty. To him, she is all he desires. In calling her "my darling," he uses a Hebrew word that has a twofold significance. On the one hand, it means that he will guard and care for her, and on the other, that he finds her sexually appealing. He, therefore, with this term of endearment, expresses "his desire to make love to her . . . [while] affirming his loving care for her."[2]

For her part, the Shulamite sees the fragrance of her perfumes as wafting symbols of her love for her husband. She expresses her satisfaction and intimates that she, too, is looking forward to the intimacies that will follow (1:13). As the banquet progresses, both Solomon and the Shulamite reminisce as they express their contentment with each other. He sees in her eyes the innocence of her person (v. 15); and she, using the rustic imagery of the woods, describes her satisfaction with him and the security she feels now that they are one (vv. 16–17).

The strain of the last few months has been great, and the Shulamite begins to feel overwhelmed by the sudden changes that have taken place in her life. She rejoices in Solomon's munificent provision and love (2:3–4), but feels the need to be strengthened for what is to follow (v. 5). She freely expresses her concerns and then shares with her groom her desire for him to have coitus with her (v. 6).

A NIGHT TO REMEMBER

The Language of Love

Each one of us needs to be loved and appreciated. This becomes more necessary the longer we are married. Expressions of endearment are essential in a growing relationship. Let us notice, therefore, the progression of lovemaking that God has seen fit to provide for us in His Word.

When they are finally alone in Solomon's bedroom, he begins by praising his wife's eyes. He comments on their color as well as what they silently convey (Song 4:1–2). Next he extols the beauty of her hair. He probably runs his fingers through it as he speaks of the captivation it holds for him. He then remarks about the whiteness, evenness, and matched symmetry of her teeth. They entrance him as she smiles.

Next, Solomon compliments his bride on her lips (4:3). He is aroused by the thought of her kisses. Their redness serves to heighten his passion, and he traces their outline with the tip of his finger. The Shulamite's cheeks are healthy and flushed with excitement. She is not a passive participant, but actively responds to her husband's words and caresses.

The fact that Solomon is also interested in the inner qualities of his wife is brought out as he traces the lines of her neck (4:4). The metaphor he uses indicates that he sees in her strength of character as well as beauty of appearance. "David's tower" was a military fortress as well as a watchtower. It was there for the protection of the nation. Solomon sees in his beloved a bulwark protecting their love from intruders. His heart safely trusts in her (Prov. 31:11).

As Solomon proceeds with foreplay, he next comes to his wife's breasts (Song 4:5–6). They are lovely and, like fawns that a person delights to show affection to by fondling, he caresses them, thereby showing his love for her (Prov. 5:19).

A Point to Ponder

It is interesting for us, in our hurried world, to notice the time taken by this couple as they prepare themselves for sexual intercourse. If you doubt the validity of this observation, take another look at verse 6. It implies continuing with their lovemaking until daybreak.

Of course, Solomon and the Shulamite are on their honeymoon and can afford to take their time. The point to be borne in mind, however, is that even when we have to rise up early the next morning, get the kids off to school, and be at the office on time, we should not hurry through our lovemaking.

The Importance of Timing

As Solomon is expressing his love for his wife, he senses that something is not right (Song 4:7–9). She appears to be momentarily distracted. Instead of complaining of her lack of interest (which would have shown his lack of understanding) or her possible fear of giving herself to him (which would have been unnatural for someone who is mature, but quite to be expected by those who are not), Solomon preserves the romantic atmosphere by praising her. He compliments her and in doing so, intimates that he desires her more than anything or anyone else. This reassures her.

Then, sensing emphatically that the fast-moving events of the past couple of days are the cause of his bride's temporary lapse of interest, he says in effect, "Come with me away from these things that would distract you; bring your thoughts from your home and the old, familiar surroundings, to me" (4:8). He then tells her of the effect she is having on him (v. 9). Such is his affection for her that a single look is sufficient to arouse his passions and make his heart beat faster.

In these few verses, therefore, we see the importance of a husband being in tune with his wife's needs and feelings. We see, too, how tender, loving words can reassure a spouse so that the mutual expression of their love can continue without abatement.

It's Skill that Counts

With verse 10 we come to a slight interpretive problem. The word *dod*, translated "love" in many versions, is really the word for "caress." This may be of any part of the body and for a variety of reasons.

In light of the context, however, it appears as if Solomon's bride has been far from passive while he has been arousing her. She has been caressing him. He speaks of her actions as "beautiful" and more stimulating than wine! As Solomon resumes foreplay, he praises her for her kisses (1:11). They are passionate and excite his desires for her.

It should be noted in passing that the open way in which

they share their feelings with each other indicates how wholesome their attitude is toward their sexuality. They are uninhibited in the best sense of the word.

Couples today have much to learn from Solomon and his bride. Often in counseling we have asked a frustrated wife or husband, "Well, have you told him (or her) how you feel? Have you shared with your spouse what you like or what you would like him (or her) to do?" Invariably the answer has been, "Well, we don't talk about things like that."

To such longsuffering people, we earnestly hope that the example of this Old Testament couple serves to remove the barriers of false modesty.

The Beauty of Sexual Expression

In their uninhibited lovemaking, Solomon and the Shulamite engage in a further expression of desire for each other (4:12–16). Each phrase is weighted with praise.

Solomon describes his bride as "a garden locked . . . a fountain sealed." This is at first surprising until we realize that the Hebrew word *gannah* refers to a covered or hidden place. Solomon uses this word *gannah* (so most commentators agree) to describe pictorially his bride's chastity. She is a virgin. She has kept her garden, herself, from those who might have defiled it.

With poetic praise, therefore, Solomon commends his beloved. At the same time, he gently requests her to allow him to enter her "garden."

The Shulamite responds to Solomon's words with a poetic invitation (4:16). She asks Solomon to come into her garden, (to possess her, v. 16). She pictures breezes blowing upon her garden so that its fragrance may bring him satisfaction. Solomon gently enters her. Then, after concluding his lovemaking, he assures her of his total satisfaction (5:1).

NEW VALUES VS. OLD TRADITIONS

It may at first astound us that such an explicit picture of true lovemaking is included in the Bible. If this is so, then what follows in the second half of this verse (5:1) will be even more surprising.

We read:

> Eat, friends;
> Drink and imbibe deeply, O lovers.

But who is the one speaking? And who are those being addressed?

Some writers have suggested that it was one of the wedding guests who uttered these words to the assembled guests. This would mean that he would have been watching Solomon and his bride make love. Such a view destroys the sanctity and intimacy of sex.

Others think that it is Solomon who turns and addresses his guests, inviting them to join in a night of carousal. This view, however, is also totally unsatisfactory. While drunken orgies took place in the banqueting halls of pagan kings, a context of promiscuity does *not* fit Solomon and the Shulamite's wedding night. Furthermore, it is Solomon and his bride who are being addressed.

The only plausible explanation—and one that has now been accepted by the majority of modern scholars—is that it is God who is speaking.[3] He is the One addressing the newlyweds as "lovers." But more broadly than that, He is the One who invites *all* lovers—each husband and wife—to partake of the benefits that He designed to be enjoyed within the bonds of marriage.

The fires of love, therefore, are the ones that He kindles (Song 8:6). He approves of sexual intimacy. At no time should the love of a husband and wife be regarded as anything that is carnal or depraved or unholy or unclean. God Himself delights to see us use what He has created.

The more we dwell upon this truth, the more we will come to appreciate the blessings of true marital harmony.

THERE'S MORE TO FOLLOW

This delightfully intriguing book continues by describing the relationship of Solomon and his bride. They were not perfect. They experienced times of estrangement and had to remind themselves of the importance of their priorities and their love for each other.

These periods when their differences tended to separate them were interspersed with deep, satisfying, and enriching periods of intimacy (Song 7:1–8:3). Through all of their experiences, the love of each for the other grew in its breadth as well as its depth. Even at the very end, the Shulamite is heard to be encouraging Solomon to come to her, so that they may enjoy the benefits of each other's company.

That is what marriage should be like—a husband and wife who, even after many years have passed, still love each other and want to be with one another.

In our hearts, this is what we all desire. The benefits, however, come to those who work for them. A happy, healthy sexuality is the outgrowth of the personal maturity of the couple and the way in which they have developed unity in their relationship.

This is exactly what is described in Genesis 2:24–25. Successful marriages require established maturity, the development of real unity, the enjoyment of an uninhibited sexuality, and the cultivation of personal transparency.

THE WINNING FORMULA

From the relationship of Solomon and the Shulamite, we glean several important lessons. These include:

- The need to be alone together to re-create the spontaneity of our early courtship and to enjoy each other's company. This does not have to be at an expensive holiday resort, but can be a quiet picnic in the country. (If you have children, leave them with their grandparents for a weekend or with another couple.)
- The need to share our feelings, desires, or fears, and to be forgetful of our own concerns so as to become "in tune" with what our spouse is saying. In time, you will develop the ability to understand his or her physical and emotional desires.
- The need to show affection toward one another. If you have children, let your children know that you love each other. In the privacy of your bedroom, engage in mutual, tactile contact—even if this does not always result in more intimate expressions of love.
- The need to take time to make love. Be considerate of the needs of your spouse and look upon this form of sexual expression as something that is sacred—as God-ordained and God-honoring.
- The need to see your marriage, with all of its ups and downs, as providing a context for mutual growth.

The Shulamite's reminiscences, which Solomon adapted into the form of a play, are deserving of extended study.

213

These few pages show briefly some of the ways in which practical wisdom may be gleaned form this ancient love song.

Interaction

1. Think back on your courtship. What were some of the memorable things you did? Discuss the "little things" you each did that meant so much to the one you loved. Write these down. Has there been any change? Why?

2. How may *both* husbands and wives create an atmosphere in the home that will be conducive of more intimate expressions of love?

3. Husband, in private, ask your wife what she would really like you to do (perhaps around the house or in the bedroom) that would convey to her the feeling that she is special.

4. Wife, when you are alone, ask your husband how you can make sex more enjoyable for both of you.

5. Discuss with one another the ways in which a sense of "inloveness" may be preserved and developed in your marriage.

Notes

Introduction

1. J. C. Dobson, Jr. *The Family Under Fire* (Kansas City, MO: Beacon Hill, 1976), p. 7.
2. D. A. Hubbard, *Is the Family Here to Stay?* Waco, TX: Word, 1971), p. 7. See also J. S. Bernard, *The Future of Marriage* (New York: World, 1972), p. 15; L. Casler, *Is Marriage Necessary?* (New York: Human Sciences, 1973), pp. 23ff.; D. C. Cooper, *Death of the Family* (New York: Random, 1971); and *Time* (April 2, 1976), p. 29.
3. G. N. Stanton, *Jesus of Nazareth in New Testament Preaching* (New York: Cambridge University Press, 1974), p. 117. Stanton's discussion of the place of biography in the literary milieu of the biblical world is worthy of serious consideration. An equally as capable though more radical treatment is C. H. Talbert's *What Is a Gospel?* (Philadelphia: Fortress, 1977).
4. J. S. Howson, *Companions of St. Paul* (New York: American Tract Society, n.d.), pp. 178–79.

1. Love's Many Faces

1. C. E. Macartney, *Great Women of the Bible* (Nashville: Abingdon, 1942), p. 10.
2. See C. J. Barber, *Vital Encounter* (San Bernardino, CA: Here's Life, 1979), pp. 123–32, for a further illustration of mature, uninhibited love.
3. R. deVaux, *Ancient Israel* (New York: McGraw-Hill, 1961), pp. 39–40.
4. *Nelson's Expository Dictionary of the Old Testament*, eds. M. F. Unger and W. White (Nashville: Thomas Nelson, 1980), pp. 232–34.
5. W. S. LaSor, *Great Personalities of the Old Testament* (Old Tappan, NJ: Revell, 1965), pp. 81ff.
6. W. E. Hulme, *Creative Loneliness* (Minneapolis: Augsburg, 1977), pp. 16–18.

7. F. C. Peters, "Marriage Is for Grown-ups," *Eternity* (Aug. 1973), pp. 21–23.

2. Second Time Around

1. K. Wiebe, *Alone: A Widow's Search for Joy* (Wheaton, IL: Tyndale, 1976), pp. 11–12.
2. deVaux, *Ancient Israel*, pp. 470–73, 490–95.
3. God's involvement in the events behind the scenes has been covered in my exposition entitled *Ruth: A Story of God's Grace* (Neptune, NJ: Loizeaux, 1989), pp. 55–60.
4. See C. A. MacKinnon, *Sexual Harassment of Working Women* (New Haven, CT: Yale University Press, 1979). See also C. Safran's "Sexual Harassment: The View from the Top," *Redbook Magazine* (Mar. 1981), pp. 45ff., 49ff.
5. G. C. Morgan, *Living Messages of the Books of the Bible* (Grand Rapids: Baker, 1982), pp. 34–36.

3. Uncommon Qualities

1. The New American Standard Bible and other versions translate this phrase "a mighty man of wealth." This seems unlikely. The same expression is used of Jephthah, Gideon's illegitimate son, *after* he had been disinherited by his brothers (Judg. 11:1), and of the poor widow Ruth (cf., Ruth 3:11, translated "excellence" in the NASB). Furthermore, everyone had just come through several years of famine. The rich would have lost much of their wealth. The general poverty of the people receives tacit confirmation from the elders and the people, for in Ruth 4:11 they express their wish that Boaz will "gain wealth" in Ephrathah.
2. Pious Israelites would not use the name *Yahweh* without good cause. *El* and *Elohim* were the more common names for God and did not have the same covenantal connotations.
3. See Barber, *Ruth*, pp. 51ff.
4. D. B. MacDonald, *Hebrew Literary Genius* (Fenwick, NY: Russell, 1960), p. 122.
5. The words of the foreman intimate that Ruth, being a foreigner *and* a widow, is not worth Boaz' time and attention. (See Barber, *Ruth*, pp. 58–60.) Boaz accepts the information, but does not adopt his servant's system of values.

4. A Matter of Priorities

1. S. Vanauken, *A Severe Mercy* (San Francisco: Harper and Row, 1977), pp. 42–43.
2. W. J. Deane, *Samuel and Saul: Their Lives and Times* (London: Nesbit, n.d.), p. 213.
3. See C. J. Barber, *Your Marriage Can Last a Lifetime* (Nashville: Thomas Nelson, 1989), pp. 107–112.
4. W. G. Blaikie, *The First Book of Samuel* (Minneapolis: Klock and Klock, 1978), pp. 7–8.
5. Barber, *Your Marriage Can Last a Lifetime*, pp. 115–63.
6. See C. J. Barber and J. D. Carter, *Always a Winner* (Ventura, CA: Regal, 1977), pp. 13–17.
7. See J. D. Pentecost, *Things to Come* (Grand Rapids: Zondervan, 1958), pp. 433–45, for a discussion of the theocracy in ancient Israel.
8. Blaikie, *First Book of Samuel*, pp. 20–21; Barber and Carter, *Always a Winner*, pp. 13–17.
9. Deane, *Samuel and Saul*, p. 11.
10. Ibid.

5. Differences in Values

1. See "Throwaway Marriages," *U.S. News and World Report* (Jan. 13, 1975), pp. 45ff.; and "Throwaway Husbands, Wives and Lovers," *Human Behavior* (Dec. 1975), pp. 65–69.
2. Macartney, *Women of the Old Testament*, p. 161.
3. W. F. Albright, *Archaeology and the Religion of Israel* (Baltimore, MD: Johns Hopkins University Press, 1953), p. 114, claims that this was definitely not an idol. However, he offers no proof in support of his assertion.
4. N. Lofts, *Women of the Old Testament* (London: Low, 1950), p. 115.
5. Ibid, pp. 117–18.
6. A. Kuyper, *Women of the Old Testament* (Grand Rapids: Zondervan, 1931), p. 110.
7. R. F. Horton, *Women of the Old Testament* (New York: Whittaker, 1899), p. 168.
8. Ibid., p. 170.
9. Lofts, *Women of the Old Testament*, p. 121.
10. Ibid.

11. L. A. Banks, *Great Portraits of the Bible* (New York: Eaton and Mains, 1903), pp. 249–51.

6. Keeping Things Honest

1. Kuyper, *Women of the Old Testament*, p. 106.
2. Not to be confused with Mount Carmel in northern Israel overlooking the Bay of Acre. The region mentioned in 1 Samuel 25 was in southern Judah (Josh. 15:55; 1 Sam. 15:12; 2 Chron. 26:10), and is situated nine miles southeast of Hebron.
3. The feast he gave was "like the feast of a king" (cf. Est. 1; Dan. 5). See F. Josephus, *Antiquities of the Jews*, VI: 15: 6–7.
4. David's anger is expressed in the literal rendering of the Hebrew text found in the margin of some Bibles.
5. Blaikie, *First Book of Samuel*, p. 385.
6. Abigail believes that David is God's theocratic representative. It is, therefore, appropriate for her to make requests of him.
7. Banks, *Great Portraits of the Bible*, pp. 240–41.
8. J. Kitto, *Daily Bible Illustrations* (Grand Rapids: Kregel, 1981), I: 577–78.

7. Prescription for Recovery

1. H. W. Hertzberg, *1 and 2 Samuel* (Louisville, KY: Westminster/John Knox, 1964), p. 309.
2. R. Patai, *Family, Love and the Bible* (New York: Doubleday, 1960), pp. 145–46. (David was about fifty years old at the time; Bathsheba was probably much younger.) Recently, students at the Old Dominion University were asked to evaluate the maturity level of those who engaged in extramarital affairs. They found them, in general, to be immature, lacking a sense of worth, and acting out their frustrations or feelings of inferiority. Not all of this was true of David, but he could easily have felt frustrated with the affairs of state, with the result that he handled the temptation as a diversion.
3. S. R. Driver, *Notes on the Hebrew Text and the Topography of the Books of Samuel* (New York: Oxford University Press, 1966), p. 289. He claims that verse 4 is a circumstantial clause defining the state of Bathsheba at the time David had sexual intercourse with her. Her bathing was to purify herself from ceremonial defilement incurred during menstruation.
4. To "wash your feet" is thought by some to be a Semitic euphemism for sexual intercourse. J. Mauchline, *1 and 2 Samuel* (Grand

Rapids: Eerdmans, 1971), p. 249, says: "[David's] instruction to Uriah to go home and wash his feet (v. 8) must have more meaning than is explicitly expressed. It is sometimes maintained that the word *feet* is a euphemism for the male organ" (see Ruth 3:4, 7).

5. Kitto, *Daily Bible Illustrations*, I: 766–67.

8. Key to Success

1. J. Michener, *Sayonara* (New York: Random, 1954), p. 17.
2. Ibid., p. 52.
3. This is estimated on the basis of thirty days to the month; the Persian penchant for beginning time from the first of the year; the probability that each region or district of the 127 provinces would send at least one finalist to the beauty contest; and that if the contest lasted a full year, there would have been at least 360 new young girls to be accommodated in the palace.
4. Deduced from the writings of Eastern religions as well as the established procedures of harems. See. J Dolinger, *Behind Harem Walls* (London: Redman, 1960).
5. Adapted from A. Maslow's *Toward a Psychology of Being* (New York: Van Nostrand, 1968), pp. 41–43.

9. The Search for Common Values

1. The case of Marie Stopes, April 6, 1931.
2. C. C. Young, *Love and Fame*, VI: 1: 65.
3. H. Rowland, *Love Letters of a Cynic*, p. 120.
4. S. Smiles, *Thrift* (London: Murray, 1875), p. 91.
5. G. C. Morgan, *Hosea: The Heart and the Holiness of God* (London: Marshall, Morgan and Scott, 1948), pp. 12–13.

10. Is Real Unity Possible in Marriage?

1. W. Barclay, *Gospel of Matthew* (Louisville, KY: Westminster/John Knox, 1958), p. 9.
2. She was not sinless, but uprightness of life caused her to merit special favor from God. The word translated "highly favored" *(kecharitomēnē)* is a perfect passive participle meaning "to be endowed with grace."
3. J. Bishop, *The Day Christ Was Born* (San Francisco: Harper and Row, 1960), p. 23.
4. A. Whyte, *Bible Characters: New Testament* (Grand Rapids: Zondervan, n.d.), p. 121.

5. The imperfect tense of the verb means that Joseph *"was not know-ing her* until after she gave birth to her firstborn Son" (Matt. 1:25). Then he and Mary enjoyed normal conjugal relations.
6. C. H. Spurgeon, *The Gospel of the Kingdom* (Pasadena, CA: Pilgrim, 1978), p. 3.
7. Bishop, *The Day Christ Was Born*, p. 1.
8. See the article entitled "Brothers of Our Lord" in the *New Unger's Bible Dictionary* (Chicago: Moody, 1989), p. 186.

11. The Value of a Good Wife

1. For a separate assessment of Pilate, see Barber, *Vital Encounter*, pp. 97–109.
2. Whyte, *Bible Characters: New Testament*, pp. 84–85.
3. Reference may be made to the following writers for historical infor-mation pertaining to this period of Roman history: Dio Cassius' *Roman History;* Seutonius' *Tiberius;* Tacitus' *Annals;* Appian's *Roman History;* Plutarch's *Lives of Famous Men;* Seneca's *Epistulae Morales.* In addition, readers will find J. Carcopino's *Daily Life in Ancient Rome* (New Haven, CT: Yale University Press, 1966), most revealing.
4. P. L. Maier, *Pontius Pilate* (Wheaton, IL: Tyndale, 1981). While differing in some particulars from the views expressed herein, Maier provides a masterful reconstruction of Pilate's life.
5. F. Josephus, *Wars of the Jews*, I; II; V: 10; and his *Antiquities of the Jews*, XV; XVIII. See also Philo's *De Legatione ad Gaium*, XXIII:159ff.; and his *In Flaccum*, I: 1ff. Both these writers de-scribe Pilate's blunders from a strongly Jewish point of view.
6. I recommend a careful reading of P. A. Cedar's *7 Keys to Maximum Communication* (Wheaton, IL: Tyndale, 1980).
7. Vanauken, *A Severe Mercy*, pp. 39–40.

12. Ahead of Their Time

1. A partial explanation has been attempted in my book *Your Mar-riage Can Last a Lifetime.*
2. For a description of the times, see Suetonious' *Claudius*, X: 25; Josephus' *Antiquities of the Jews*, XIX: 5; XX: 1, 2; Dio Cassius' *Roman History*, LX: 8; Orosius' *History*, VII: 6; Tacitus' *Annals*, XII: 66–67, from which sources the information in this chapter has been reconstructed.

3. A. C. McGiffert, *The Apostolic Age* (Edinburgh: Clark, 1921), p. 428.

4. R. C. H. Lenski, *The Interpretation of the Acts of the Apostles* (Minneapolis: Augsburg, 1962), p. 768.

5. See Suetonius; *Claudius*, 25. Dio Cassius (LX: 6), however, contradicts Suetonious and the testimony of Scripture. See W. M. Ramsay, *St. Paul the Traveller and Roman Citizen* (Grand Rapids: Baker, 1951), p. 254, for a concise explanation of the events.

6. W. Barclay, *Letters to the Corinthians* (Louisville, KY: Westminster/John Knox, 1956), pp. 1, 3.

7. D. E. Hiebert, *Personalities Around Paul* (Chicago: Moody, 1973), pp. 40–41.

8. M. Horner, "For Lots of Working Women, 'Price of Success Is Too High'," *U.S. News and World Report*, (Nov. 23, 1981), p. 76; see also "Letters to the Editor," *Saturday Review* (Mar. 1970), pp. 23–24; C. Tavris and T. Jayaratne, "Redbook Survey: How Women Really Feel About the 'New Feminism'," *Redbook* (Jan. 1973), pp. 156–57; "Wife Leaves Mate, Baby for Career," *L.A. Times,* May 16, 1973; "Reflections on Women's Lib," *Christianity Today* (Jan. 3, 1975), pp. 25–26; M. M. Ferree, "The Confused American Housewife," *Psychology Today* (Sept. 1966), pp. 76–80; and B. G. Harrison, "Why Some Women Feel Secure—and So Many Don't," *Redbook* (Mar. 1977), pp. 48ff.

9. A. T. Robertson, *Types of Preachers in the New Testament* (New York: Doran, 1922), pp. 68, 70.

13. Love Comes Softly

1. For a detailed explanation of these orientalisms, see F. Delitzsch, *Commentary on the Song of Songs and Ecclesiastes* (Grand Rapids: Eerdmans, n.d.), pp. 1–176; J. C. Dillow, *Solomon on Sex* (Nashville: Thomas Nelson, 1977); and S. C. Glickman, *A Song for Lovers* (Downers Grove, IL: InterVarsity, 1976).

2. Dillow, *Solomon on Sex*, p. 21.

3. *Ryrie Study Bible* (Chicago: Moody, 1978), pp. 1006.